The Sugar Savvy Squa

By Catherine Sabatina

Disclaimer:

The information provided in this book is intended for general informational purposes only. It is not meant to be a substitute for professional medical advice, diagnosis, or treatment. Always seek the advice of your physician or another qualified healthcare provider with any questions you may have regarding a medical condition.

The recipes and dietary recommendations presented in this book are based on research, personal experiences, and expert knowledge, but individual responses to specific foods or dietary changes may vary. Before making any significant changes to your diet or lifestyle, it is essential to consult with a registered dietitian, nutritionist, or healthcare professional, especially if you have any underlying health conditions, allergies, or specific dietary requirements.

Please note that while efforts have been made to ensure the accuracy and completeness of the information in this book, we do not guarantee that the content is free of errors or omissions. The authors, publishers, and distributors of this book disclaim any liability for any direct, indirect, or consequential loss or damage that may arise from the use or misuse of the information provided herein.

It is essential to use your best judgment and individual discretion when following any recipes or nutritional recommendations in this book. Remember that each person's nutritional needs are unique, and what works for one individual may not be suitable for another.

Disclaimer for Sugar-Free Fortnight:

The information provided in the Sugar-Free Fortnight campaign is for general informational purposes only and is not intended as medical advice. It is not a substitute for professional medical advice, diagnosis, or treatment. Always seek the advice of your physician or another qualified health provider with any questions you may have regarding a medical condition.

The Sugar-Free Fortnight campaign promotes reducing sugar intake for a healthier lifestyle. However, individual dietary needs may vary, and it is essential to consult with a registered dietitian or healthcare professional before making significant changes to your diet, especially if you have any existing health conditions.

Participation in the Sugar-Free Fortnight campaign is entirely voluntary, and any actions taken based on the information provided are at the participant's own risk. The organizers of the campaign are not responsible for any adverse effects or consequences resulting from the implementation of the advice or recommendations provided.

The Sugar-Free Fortnight campaign may include testimonials and success stories from participants. These individual experiences are not indicative of guaranteed results, and individual outcomes may vary.

By participating in the Sugar-Free Fortnight campaign, you acknowledge that you have read and understood this disclaimer and agree to assume full responsibility for your health decisions and actions.

If you experience any adverse reactions or concerns during the Sugar-Free Fortnight campaign, please seek immediate medical attention and discontinue participation.

Hello From Catherine!

The Hidden Perils of Excessive Sugar Consumption

"Today, I want to address a pressing issue that affects many of us: the dangers of excessive sugar consumption. In our modern society, we find ourselves surrounded by cheap, processed foods laden with sugar, processed meats, mountains of sodium... I aim to shed light on why these foods are so prevalent, why we are drawn to them, and how our frequent snacking habits lead to severe sugar spikes and crashes.

Furthermore, I will explain the role of insulin, hormones, and satiety signals, and how an imbalanced diet rich in complex carbohydrates can impact our overall health and well-being. This book is not just about providing delicious recipes; it aims to empower readers with knowledge about the profound impacts of sugar on our bodies. Understanding how sugar influences our health will enable us to make informed choices that support a thriving and nourished life.

The focus is on education, learning about the science behind sugar's detrimental effects, from its role in inflammation to its contribution to chronic diseases. Armed with this knowledge, we'll take back the reins of our lives, no longer fooled by the manipulative tactics of food companies.

Each recipe in this book is carefully crafted to offer not only a delightful dining experience but also a step towards healing and renewal. We'll discover the joy of creating flavourful dishes that nourish our bodies, free from harmful additives and excessive sugar present in store-bought options.

But this journey is not just about recipes and the food on our plates. In my Sugar Savvy book, I take a holistic approach to wellness. I believe that true health goes beyond what we eat; it encompasses the whole spectrum of our lifestyle.

In the pages of this book, we'll learn about the importance of exercise, not just for physical fitness but also for mental well-being. We'll explore the significance of quality sleep, fresh air, and mindful breathing, as these aspects profoundly impact our vitality.

Moreover, I share tips about taking your investment in health to the next level. We'll delve into the world of glucose monitors to gain a deeper understanding of our blood sugar levels and how they relate to our overall health. We'll consider seeking guidance from nutritionists to receive personalized advice that aligns with our unique needs and goals.

For those who desire even more in-depth knowledge and customization, I introduce the concept of Zoe Science Nutrition personalized plans. This groundbreaking science enables us to tailor our diets to our bodies' specific responses, paving the way for enhanced well-being.

As we embark on this journey towards sugar savvy living, we may discover an insatiable desire to invest in our health even further. And that's what I hope for every reader of this book - to embrace health as the real wealth.

This is just the beginning of a transformative path. As we savour the delicious, nutrient-dense meals from this book, we'll nourish not only our bodies but also our minds and spirits. Each wholesome meal will fill our hearts with hope, guiding us towards a healthier, more vibrant future.

Together, we will unleash hope onto our plates and into our bodies. With every step we take, we'll rewrite our health narrative and become the architects of our lives. So, let's embrace a lifestyle that not only tastes good but also feels good.

By nourishing ourselves with savvy food choices and adopting healthier habits, we will not only enrich our lives but also inspire others to do the same. So, join me in savouring the gift of a healthier and happier life, where health truly becomes our greatest wealth."
-Catherine

Introduction

Within the realm of nutrition, a universal solution capable of ensuring optimal health for all remains elusive. Our intricate genetic makeup, unique metabolic processes, and individualized lifestyles collectively determine our distinct reactions to various foods. Navigating our personalized dietary requirements proves to be a formidable challenge, often necessitating comprehensive blood analyses or expert guidance from qualified nutritionists to unveil our body's specific needs.

The crux of the matter lies not in pursuing an intricate path but in adopting a discerning, broad-based approach that advocates for overall wellness. A pivotal step within everyone's reach involves a significant reduction or complete elimination of ultra-processed foods from our culinary choices. These convenient yet excessively processed alternatives abound in refined sugars, detrimental fats, and synthetic additives, offering scant nutritional value. Astute consumers discern that such edibles yield no benefits and can, in fact, impair our health when consumed excessively.

Food conglomerates wield shrewd marketing strategies, employing alluring visuals and captivating slogans to entice consumers, particularly impressionable children. However, the sagacious consumer remains impervious to these enticements, dedicating time to peruse labels and scrutinize ingredients before making selections. They are aware that despite the captivating packaging, some of these products are ill-suited for their well-being.

Embracing fleeting dietary trends or fads often proves to be misleading. Discerning individuals recognize that such vogues might not align with their distinct necessities, potentially leading to unnecessary constraints or dietary imbalances. Instead, they prioritize a well-rounded regimen enriched with whole, nutrient-dense victuals such as vegetables, fruits, lean proteins, and wholesome fats.

While certain diets or nutritional paradigms may indeed yield benefits for certain individuals, those who are astute understand that our bodies are intricate systems. The regimen that yields success for one might prove futile for another. Prioritizing whole foods and curtailing consumption of heavily processed commodities emerges as a judicious choice for safeguarding well-being.

Ultimately, nutritional acumen involves assuming control over our health and vitality while circumventing the snares set by cunning marketing strategies and disingenuous practices within the food industry. It signifies maintaining awareness, making conscious decisions, and seeking tailored guidance as necessary. Through nutritional discernment, we can adopt a sustainable, diverse, and balanced diet that stands as the bedrock for enduring health and energy.

Exploring Historical Influences on Dietary Habits:

Throughout the annals of time, our dietary patterns have undergone profound transformations under the sway of diverse factors such as cultural shifts, societal progress, and technological innovations. The tapestry of our dietary challenges is woven from myriad historical occurrences, shaping our contemporary culinary habits. Let's delve into key aspects of this historical tapestry:

Agricultural Revolution: The epochal shift from nomadic hunter-gatherer societies to agrarian communities heralded a momentous transition in our dietary habits. The cultivation of crops and domestication of animals introduced novel staples, altering our traditional sources of sustenance.

Industrial Revolution: The advent of the industrial age introduced methods for processing and preserving food. While these breakthroughs bolstered food availability, they also engendered the proliferation of refined flours, canned goods, and processed meats, which might lack vital nutrients.

Technological Progress: Strides in transportation and refrigeration ushered in an era of expanded food distribution, granting access to an array of options year-round. However, this convenience paralleled the introduction of more processed and less nourishing choices.

Marketing and Advertising: The ascendancy of mass media and consumerism in the 20th century birthed pervasive marketing campaigns for processed foods, sugary beverages, and snacks. These promotional endeavours exerted substantial influence on our dietary inclinations.

Fast Food Culture: In the wake of World War II, the fast-food industry emerged, focusing on expedient, affordable, yet often less wholesome fare. Fast food rapidly ingrained itself into many diets, moulding our collective eating practices.

Hectic Lifestyles: The exigencies of contemporary life frequently led to time constraints, fostering reliance on convenient but occasionally less nutritious edibles.

Food Policies and Subsidies: Governmental food policies and subsidies can tilt in favour of specific crops, such as corn and soy, prevalent in processed foods and sugary drinks. This dynamic can impact the accessibility and affordability of healthier alternatives.

Taste Preferences: Our gustatory inclinations have evolved to favour flavours like sweet, salty, and fatty, traits often prevalent in processed and less nutritious victuals. These preferences can be moulded by cultural norms and exposure.

Food Environment: Our surroundings, encompassing the availability of grocery outlets, eateries, and food marketing, wield substantial influence over our dietary selections.

Acknowledging the historical backdrop and grasping the intricate factors sculpting our eating patterns empowers us to make enlightened decisions. By adopting well-balanced diets rich in nutrients, cantered on whole foods, fruits, vegetables, and lean proteins, we can proactively cultivate healthier eating habits, thereby prioritizing our holistic well-being.

My Mission

"In a world filled with ever-changing diet trends, the "Sugar Savvy Squad" book offers a refreshing perspective by nurturing understanding instead of promoting fads. It's my mission to assist individuals in gradually reducing their reliance on ultra-processed foods and excessive sugar consumption. Rather than dictating how to live, my aim is to provide education that empowers readers to make informed decisions about their dietary choices. Recognizing that everyone is on their own unique journey, I offer insights and knowledge to support a transition towards healthier eating habits. Ultimately, the goal is to equip individuals with the tools they need to navigate their relationship with food and make adult decisions that align with their well-being.

Here's how the book provides insight into the complexities of modern diets and a path to better health:

Balanced Perspective on Sugar: Sugar isn't entirely negative, but overconsumption, especially in ultra-processed foods, can contribute to various modern health issues.

Understanding Modern Ailments: By shedding light on the role of sugar and processed foods, the book connects the dots between our diets and modern-day physical and mental afflictions.

Evolution vs. Diet Disruption: Explaining how our brains have evolved over time while our bodies are adapted to ancestral diets, the book highlights how processed foods and excessive sugar consumption disrupt this harmony.

Unveiling the Fake Food Issue: The book explores how our bodies struggle with processing "fake" foods, leading to discomfort, mood swings, and health problems.

Return to Cooking: Encouraging a return to home cooking, the book emphasizes that preparing meals from scratch helps us avoid hidden sugars and unknown additives."

Chapter 1

Sugar, the White Stuff that's simply EVERYWHERE!

Sugar isn't all bad; in fact, it's necessary for our bodies to function properly. When we consume carbohydrates from food, they are processed into glucose, which our cells use as fuel and energy. The problem is we're eating way too much of it!

There are two main types of sugar in our diet: glucose and fructose.

Glucose is the primary source of energy for our cells. When we consume sugar or foods with carbohydrates, our bodies break them down into glucose. This glucose is then absorbed into the bloodstream and transported to cells throughout the body, where it is used for energy production. Any excess glucose can be stored in the liver and muscles as glycogen for later use.

Fructose is another type of sugar primarily found in fruits, some vegetables, and added sugars. When we consume fructose, our liver metabolizes it. The liver converts fructose into glucose or stores it as glycogen for later use. However, excessive fructose intake can overwhelm the liver's capacity to metabolize it, leading to the conversion of fructose into fat molecules. This can contribute to liver fat accumulation and potential health issues.

Unlike glucose, fructose has a one-track path to the liver and can lead to problems when consumed in excess, especially in processed foods lacking the natural fibre found in fruits and vegetables that would otherwise protect our bodies from its direct impact.

Being mindful of our sugar intake and making informed choices can help us maintain a balanced and healthy diet. Including natural sources of sugar from whole foods, such as fruits and dairy, can provide essential nutrients and fibre that support overall health. On the other hand, reducing added sugars and highly processed foods that contain excessive fructose can promote better liver function and overall well-being. By understanding how our bodies process sugar and its different forms, we can make more conscious decisions about our dietary choices and work towards a healthier lifestyle.

Science stuff!

When carbohydrates enter the body, they fall into one of the three major macronutrient categories: carbs, fats, and proteins. Carbs are made up of chains of glucose. As we consume carbs, the body absorbs glucose, leading to a rise in blood glucose and insulin levels. Insulin plays a crucial role by allowing cells to use glucose for immediate energy needs. Any excess glucose that is not used at that moment is stored as glycogen.

The process of breaking down carbs into glucose occurs in two major forms: amylopectin and amylose. These glucose molecules are then restructured into glycogen and stored in the liver. During periods of fasting, such as when we sleep, the body utilizes glycogen and converts it back into glucose to maintain essential bodily functions.

Our ability to store and release glycogen ensures that we don't have to eat continuously to sustain energy levels. However, with the availability of cheap and easily accessible food in today's modern world, we often find ourselves deviating from our natural eating patterns.

In contrast, fats are metabolized differently. When we consume fats, they are directly stored in our fat cells if our glycogen stores are already full. This excessive accumulation of fat in the liver can lead to fatty liver disease and abdominal obesity. Furthermore, our triglyceride levels tend to rise, while high-density lipoprotein (HDL) levels decrease, which can negatively impact heart health.

To maintain a healthy balance, it is essential to differentiate between processed and complex carbohydrates. Complex carbs, found in fibre-rich sources like a rainbow of vegetables, provide sustained energy and keep us feeling fuller for longer. On the contrary, processed carbs, such as white bread and jam, cause rapid spikes in blood glucose and insulin levels, leading to a cycle of energy crashes and hunger pangs.

To maintain stable energy levels and avoid feeling fatigued or hypoglycaemic, it's crucial to choose nutrient-dense, fibre-rich foods that support balanced blood sugar levels. By prioritizing these food choices, we can promote optimal hormonal balance and overall well-being.

Chapter 2

Insulin and Obesity

Insulin, a natural hormone, acts as a nutrient sensor in our bodies. When we consume food, especially those high in carbohydrates, insulin levels increase, and the body absorbs glucose to use as fuel and energy. Carbohydrates break down into glucose molecules, and any excess energy is stored as glycogen in the liver.

However, the modern diet, characterized by highly processed foods and constant snacking, has led to excessive insulin spikes. This pattern of eating, coupled with a high intake of refined carbohydrates, contributes to obesity, as the body ends up storing more energy than it can handle. Consuming large quantities of sugary foods and refined carbs can lead to a cascade of health issues, including metabolic syndrome and diabetes.

As we switched from a more natural diet to one high in refined carbs and sugar in the late 70s, misinformation prevailed. Foods like avocados, nuts, olive oil, and eggs were unjustly demonized, while sugary beverages became more widely accepted.

Carbohydrates are broken down into glucose when ingested, and the body uses this glucose for immediate energy needs. Any excess glucose is converted into glycogen and stored in the liver. Our body can use this stored glycogen as a source of glucose when we are not eating, which is why we don't need to eat constantly. However, with the abundance of readily available food, we often go against our natural eating patterns.

Fats, on the other hand, are stored directly as fat in the body. When the body's glycogen storage is full, excess carbohydrates can be converted into fat, leading to fatty liver and abdominal obesity. This process also raises triglyceride levels and lowers HDL cholesterol.

It is crucial to differentiate between processed carbs and complex carbs, which are rich in fibre. Including a variety of colourful vegetables in our diet provides essential nutrients and supports stable blood sugar levels. This helps avoid sharp insulin spikes that can lead to hypoglycaemia and cravings for more food, creating a cycle of constant snacking.

Choosing whole foods and opting for a balanced diet can help us manage insulin levels and prevent excessive energy storage. By embracing a healthier approach to eating and understanding how our bodies respond to different foods, we can break free from the cycle of constant hunger and achieve a more sustainable and nourishing way of living.

Obesity is a medical condition characterized by an excessive accumulation of body fat that can have negative effects on health. It is usually measured by the body mass index (BMI), which is calculated by dividing a person's weight in kilograms by the square of their height in meters. A BMI of 30 or higher is generally considered obese. Obesity can lead to a variety of health issues, including cardiovascular disease, diabetes, and certain types of cancer.

Abdominal Obesity:

Abdominal obesity, also known as central or visceral obesity, refers to the accumulation of fat in the abdominal region. Unlike subcutaneous fat (which is found just under the skin throughout the body), visceral fat surrounds the internal organs in the abdominal cavity. It is often measured by waist circumference. Abdominal obesity is considered a significant risk factor for various health problems, including insulin resistance, metabolic syndrome, and cardiovascular disease.

Diabetes:

Diabetes mellitus, commonly known as diabetes, is a chronic metabolic disorder that affects how the body processes glucose (sugar). There are two main types of diabetes:

a. Type 1 Diabetes: This is an autoimmune condition in which the body's immune system attacks and destroys insulin-producing cells in the pancreas. People with type 1 diabetes require insulin injections or an insulin pump to regulate blood sugar levels.

b. Type 2 Diabetes: This is the most common form of diabetes and occurs when the body becomes resistant to insulin or doesn't produce enough insulin to maintain normal blood sugar levels. Type 2 diabetes is often associated with lifestyle factors such as obesity, sedentary behaviour, and poor dietary habits.

Metabolic Syndrome:

Metabolic syndrome is a cluster of risk factors that increase the likelihood of developing heart disease, stroke, and type 2 diabetes. The specific criteria for diagnosing metabolic syndrome include having three or more of the following:

a. Abdominal obesity (increased waist circumference)

b. High blood pressure (hypertension)

c. High fasting blood sugar levels

d. High triglyceride levels in the blood

e. Low levels of high-density lipoprotein (HDL) cholesterol, often referred to as "good" cholesterol

Metabolic syndrome is closely related to insulin resistance and is thought to be a result of a combination of genetic and lifestyle factors, including poor diet, lack of physical activity, and obesity.

Inflammation:

Inflammation is the body's natural response to injury or infection. When tissues are damaged, the immune system releases chemicals to help repair the area and defend against potential pathogens. However, chronic inflammation can be harmful and is associated with various diseases, including cardiovascular diseases, arthritis, and certain cancers. Obesity and metabolic syndrome are known to promote chronic low-grade inflammation in the body.

Link to High Sugar:

High sugar consumption, especially in the form of added sugars and sugary beverages, has been associated with an increased risk of obesity, abdominal obesity, type 2 diabetes, metabolic syndrome, and inflammation. When you consume a lot of sugary foods or drinks, your blood sugar levels rise rapidly, leading to an increased release of insulin. Over time, repeated spikes in blood sugar and insulin can contribute to insulin resistance, a condition in which the body's cells become less responsive to insulin's effects.

Insulin resistance is a key factor in the development of type 2 diabetes and metabolic syndrome. Additionally, excess sugar intake can contribute to weight gain and abdominal obesity, both of which are linked to an increased risk of various health issues, including cardiovascular disease.

In summary, the links between obesity, abdominal obesity, diabetes, metabolic syndrome, inflammation, and high sugar consumption are complex and interconnected. Adopting a healthy lifestyle that includes a balanced diet, regular physical activity, and weight management is crucial in reducing the risk of these conditions and promoting overall well-being.

A message from Catherine! Cracking the Sweet Trap: Why We Can't Stop at One Cookie

Sweet Temptations and the Cookie Mystery

"We've all been there – faced with a plate of cookies, and suddenly, having just one seems impossible. But why is it so hard? Let's explore the science behind sugar addiction, the reasons we can't resist another cookie, and the impact it has on us.

What Makes Sugar So Addictive?

Sugar is like a secret code to our brain's pleasure centre. When we eat something sweet, our brain releases a chemical called dopamine, which makes us feel happy. However, if we eat sugary stuff a lot, our brain starts getting used to it, so we need more and more sugar to feel that same happiness. It's a bit like needing a louder song to get the same excited feeling.

Why That One Cookie Doesn't Cut It

When we munch on a cookie, our body reacts in a way that makes us want more. First, sugar in the cookie gives us a quick burst of energy, but then our energy drops really low. This energy crash tricks our body into thinking we need more sugar to feel better again. Also, sugar can mess with parts of our brain that handle cravings and self-control, making it really hard to say "no" to another cookie. Plus, it can make us feel hungry even when we're not really hungry – it's like a trick our body plays on us.

Sugar's Sneaky Effects on Us

This sugar addiction isn't just about eating more cookies; it can lead to some not-so-great stuff. If we keep eating too many sugary things, we might gain weight and have a higher chance of getting sick, like having problems with our heart or getting diabetes. Also, our mood can go up and down like a roller coaster because of all the sugar. Ever felt super happy after eating a candy bar and then suddenly grumpy? That's the sugar doing its roller-coaster thing.

Breaking Free from the Sugar Spell

It might sound tough, but we can totally beat this sugar addiction! One way is to slowly eat less sugary stuff, so our brain gets used to less dopamine and doesn't keep begging for more sugar. Instead of cookies, we can try eating foods that give us energy over a longer time, like fruits, veggies, and whole grains. And when we want a cookie, taking a moment to think if we're really hungry or just craving sugar can help us make better choices.

Conclusion: Outsmarting the Sweet Temptation

So, the next time you're faced with a plate of cookies and wonder why you can't stop at one, remember that your brain is wired to love sugar a little too much. But armed with this knowledge, you can outsmart the sugar trap. By understanding how sugar affects your body and mind, you can take control, make healthier choices, and enjoy the sweetness of life without falling into the sugar addiction spiral."

Chapter 3

Basal Metabolic Rate and Calorie Counting

Counting calories and fixating solely on caloric intake can lead to nutrient deficiencies, as it disregards the vital importance of consuming a well-balanced diet rich in essential vitamins, minerals, and macronutrients. When individuals obsess over restricting their calorie intake without considering the nutritional value of their food choices, they risk depriving their bodies of essential nutrients necessary for overall health and well-being.

Moreover, resorting to extreme measures, such as starving ourselves to achieve weight loss, can have detrimental effects on our basal metabolic rate (BMR), which represents the energy our bodies use while at rest, excluding exercise. Drastically reducing calorie intake signals the body that it is experiencing a period of famine, prompting a survival response that slows down the metabolic rate to conserve energy. This ancient adaptation once helped our ancestors endure times of scarcity; however, in the context of our modern diets and lifestyle, this response can prove counterproductive and hinder long-term weight loss efforts.

Hormonal regulation in our bodies plays a pivotal role in managing weight and overall health. Hormones like insulin and leptin directly influence hunger, appetite, and energy storage. It is essential to understand that the body prioritizes maintaining hormonal balance over simply tallying calories. For instance, when we consume refined carbohydrates and sugars, they cause rapid spikes in blood glucose and insulin levels. Elevated insulin levels signal the body to store excess glucose as fat, leading to weight gain. Conversely, when we opt for nutrient-dense foods that support stable blood sugar levels, insulin remains steady, contributing to a healthier body composition.

The basal metabolic rate (BMR) is a critical component of our total energy expenditure. While exercise can boost energy consumption, it typically accounts for only a fraction of our daily calorie burn. The body requires a significant amount of energy for fundamental functions, including maintaining body temperature, supporting heart function, and sustaining brain activity. Even during rest, our BMR plays a substantial role in our overall daily energy needs, often amounting to around 1800 calories or more.

Relying solely on exercise to create a calorie deficit may not be the most efficient approach for weight loss. Instead, adopting a well-rounded diet with appropriate caloric intake and prioritizing nutrient-dense foods is key. A balanced diet ensures that our bodies receive the essential nutrients required for optimal functioning while providing sustained energy throughout the day.

In conclusion, comprehending the intricate hormonal responses within our bodies to the foods we consume is paramount for successful weight management and overall well-being. Rather than fixating on calorie counting alone, it is crucial to emphasize the importance of nutrient-dense foods, supporting hormonal balance, and maintaining a well-balanced diet to achieve sustainable weight management and overall health.

Chapter 4

Cereal or Steak?

A breakfast consisting of steak, eggs, and broccoli is likely to keep you full for a longer time compared to a breakfast of cereal and orange juice due to several scientific reasons:

Protein Content: Steak and eggs are rich sources of high-quality protein. Protein takes longer to digest than carbohydrates, and it has a higher thermic effect of food, meaning it requires more energy to be metabolized. This leads to increased satiety and a feeling of fullness. A study published in the American Journal of Clinical Nutrition found that high-protein breakfasts were associated with reduced hunger and increased fullness compared to high-carbohydrate breakfasts.

Fibre Content: Broccoli is a fibrous vegetable, providing dietary fibre. Fibre adds bulk to your meals, slowing down the digestion process and promoting a feeling of fullness. A study published in the journal Nutrition Reviews demonstrated that dietary fibre intake can influence satiety and reduce overall calorie intake.

Blood Sugar Stability: Cereal and orange juice are high in simple carbohydrates and sugars, which can lead to rapid spikes in blood sugar levels, followed by crashes.

These fluctuations can trigger hunger and cravings shortly after consuming the meal. In contrast, the combination of protein, healthy fats, and fibre in the steak, eggs, and broccoli breakfast leads to a slower release of glucose into the bloodstream, promoting more stable blood sugar levels.

Hormonal Response: The consumption of carbohydrates, especially in the form of high-sugar foods, triggers the release of insulin. Insulin promotes the uptake of glucose by cells and signals the body to store excess energy as fat. This process can lead to feelings of hunger and cravings for more carbohydrates. In contrast, protein-rich meals like steak and eggs stimulate the release of hormones that promote satiety and reduce appetite, as mentioned in a study published in the American Journal of Clinical Nutrition.

Nutrient Density: Steak, eggs, and broccoli are nutrient-dense foods, meaning they provide a wide range of essential vitamins, minerals, and nutrients per calorie. Nutrient-dense foods are more satisfying to the body's nutrient requirements, reducing the urge to seek out additional food.

In conclusion, a breakfast consisting of steak, eggs, and broccoli is more likely to keep you feeling full and satisfied for a longer time compared to a breakfast of cereal and orange juice. The combination of protein, fiber, stable blood sugar levels, and nutrient density contributes to enhanced satiety and reduced hunger, supporting a balanced and nutritious start to the day.

A breakfast of cereal with low-fat milk and orange juice can lead to a different physiological response compared to the steak, eggs, and broccoli breakfast. Here are some reasons why:

High Glycaemic Load: Cereal and orange juice are high-glycaemic foods, meaning they cause a rapid increase in blood glucose levels. The high sugar content in orange juice and processed carbohydrates in cereal can lead to a quick spike in blood sugar, followed by a subsequent drop, leaving you feeling hungry shortly after the meal. A study published in The American Journal of Clinical Nutrition demonstrated that high-glycaemic meals can result in increased hunger and cravings.

Lack of Satiety-Boosting Nutrients: Cereal with low-fat milk and orange juice lacks significant protein and fibre content. Protein and fibre are essential for promoting satiety and reducing appetite. Without these satiety-boosting nutrients, you may feel less satisfied and more likely to seek out additional snacks or meals shortly after eating.

Insulin Response: The high sugar content in orange juice and the carbohydrate-rich cereal can lead to a surge in insulin secretion. This insulin response can promote fat storage and disrupt the body's ability to utilize stored fat for energy. Research published in Diabetes Care suggests that high insulin levels can hinder fat metabolism and contribute to increased feelings of hunger and weight gain.

Nutrient Profile: While cereals often contain added vitamins and minerals, they may lack the full spectrum of nutrients found in whole, nutrient-dense foods like steak and broccoli. A study published in the journal Nutrients highlighted the importance of consuming nutrient-dense foods to meet the body's nutritional requirements and maintain satiety.

In summary, a breakfast of cereal with low-fat milk and orange juice can lead to rapid fluctuations in blood sugar levels, reduced satiety, and increased hunger shortly after eating. The lack of protein, fibre, and nutrient density in this breakfast option may leave you feeling unsatisfied and more inclined to consume additional food throughout the day. Choosing a balanced breakfast like steak, eggs, and broccoli that provides protein, fibre, and a range of essential nutrients can support better appetite control and overall well-being.

Chapter 5

Cindy

Once upon a Monday morning, in a bustling city, lived a woman named Cindy. Like most people, she had a busy modern life, juggling work, gym sessions, and the never-ending demands of home. Cindy believed in the conventional wisdom of eating a low-fat, high-carb breakfast to start her day on a "healthy" note.

One fine morning, Cindy rolled out of bed and made her way to the kitchen. Instead of grabbing a wholesome breakfast, she opted for a giant bowl of sugary cereal, topped with low-fat milk to keep it "healthy," and a glass of orange juice to wash it down. Little did she know that her carb-heavy breakfast would set the tone for her day.

As Cindy devoured her colourful cereal, she felt an instant rush of energy. "This is the life!" she thought, feeling like a kid again with her sugary delight. But little did she realize that this energy boost was short-lived, like a sugar-coated rollercoaster.

By mid-morning, the sugar rush started to wane, leaving Cindy feeling irritable and low on energy. She found herself daydreaming during a work presentation, only to be snapped back to reality with a nudge from her co-worker. "Sorry, just lost in thought," she stammered, trying to hide her carb-induced brain fog.

As the clock struck noon, Cindy found herself in the office meeting room, trying her best to stay engaged in the discussion. But her carb crash had other plans for her. As her colleague presented a detailed report on quarterly earnings, Cindy felt her eyelids drooping like lead weights. She desperately tried to stifle a yawn, pretending to nod in agreement with every point made, but her head bobbed up and down uncontrollably. She was moments away from dozing off right there at the conference table!

Suddenly, her boss called on her for input, and Cindy jolted awake with a start. "Uh, yes, great numbers! I mean, uh, well done," she mumbled, hoping nobody noticed her momentary nap in the middle of the meeting.

Back at her desk, Cindy's energy levels continued to fluctuate. One moment she was hyper and chatty, and the next she was dragging her feet, desperately seeking a quick pick-me-up. She found herself running to the office vending machine, on a mission to find a chocolate bar to curb her persistent carb cravings.

In the afternoon, Cindy decided to hit the gym for a much-needed workout. However, her carb-heavy breakfast left her feeling sluggish and unmotivated. She struggled through her exercise routine, feeling more like a zombie than a fitness enthusiast.

As the workday neared its end, Cindy's hunger pangs returned with a vengeance. She raided the office pantry in search of snacks, devouring anything she could find – from cookies to chips. The carb cravings seemed insatiable, leading her on a wild scavenger hunt for more sweet and starchy treats.

Exhausted and a little frazzled, Cindy finally made it home. She wanted a comforting dinner, but the carb-induced rollercoaster had taken its toll on her appetite and mood. She slumped on the couch, craving something quick and easy.

As the clock struck bedtime, Cindy lay awake, feeling wired and tired at the same time. Her carb-filled day had left her body in a state of confusion, unsure of when to feel awake or sleepy.

That night, as Cindy lay in bed, she couldn't help but reflect on her carb-filled day. The promise of a "healthy" low-fat, high-carb breakfast had left her feeling like a hangry, sleepy, and frazzled mess. It was time for her to reconsider her approach to eating and embrace a more balanced and nutrient-rich way of fuelling her body.

And so, as the sun rose on a new day, Cindy vowed to leave the carb-coaster behind and embark on a journey to discover the power of nourishing, wholesome foods that would keep her energized, satisfied, and ready to conquer the world – one bite at a time.

Chapter 6
The Poor Little Pancreas

Once upon a time, in the vibrant town of Bodyville, the organs and systems lived harmoniously, working together to ensure the well-being of the townspeople. At the heart of this community was the magnificent Pancreas Palace, home to the diligent Pancreas, the overseer of sugar regulation.

The Pancreas, a hardworking individual, diligently produced a remarkable hormone called Insulin. Insulin played a crucial role in maintaining the balance of sugar in the bloodstream, acting as a key to unlock the doors of the cells, allowing glucose to enter and provide energy to the townspeople.

However, a series of events unfolded that put an immense strain on the Pancreas and pushed it to its limits. It all began when an enchanting place called Sweetland emerged on the outskirts of Bodyville. Sweetland was a land filled with tantalizing cakes, tempting treats, and deceptive low-fat foods that masked their high sugar content.

The townspeople, enticed by the allure of Sweetland's offerings, indulged in these sugar-laden delights without realizing the consequences that lay ahead. As they consumed these delectable treats, the glucose from the sugar flooded their bloodstream, setting off a chain reaction within the town's cellular community.

The Pancreas, tirelessly working to produce enough Insulin to manage the increasing sugar intake, found itself overwhelmed. The constant demand for Insulin became a burden too heavy to bear, leaving the Pancreas overworked and underappreciated.

Despite its best efforts, the Pancreas reached a breaking point. It felt like an overworked employee who had been underpaid for far too long. The Pancreas, exhausted and frustrated, made a bold decision—it went on strike.

With the Pancreas refusing to release sufficient Insulin, the townspeople of Bodyville faced dire consequences. Glucose, now unable to enter the cells effectively, remained trapped in the bloodstream, causing high blood sugar levels—a condition known as Hyperglycaemia.

The townspeople experienced a range of health issues as a result of the excessive sugar levels. Fatigue became a constant companion, as the cells lacked the energy they needed to function optimally. Weight gain and obesity became prevalent as excess glucose was converted into fat and stored in the Adipose Tissue, the Fat Storage Facility.

Mood swings plagued the townspeople, as the constant fluctuations in blood sugar levels caused by the excessive sugar intake led to emotional instability and irritability. Diabetes, a representation of the disrupted sugar regulation, emerged, further exacerbating the townspeople's health challenges.

As the townspeople of Bodyville grappled with the consequences of their sugar-laden indulgences, they began to realize the importance of making healthier choices. They recognized the need to reduce their intake of processed foods, particularly those misleadingly labelled as low-fat but filled with hidden sugars.

The townspeople embarked on a journey of transformation, embracing a new way of living. They turned to nourishing whole foods, including fruits, vegetables, lean organic meats, and fish. They understood the significance of incorporating spelte grains like spelt and rye into their diets, as these grains provided more nutrients and fibre compared to refined wheat products.

As the townspeople shifted towards a more natural and balanced diet, the effects were remarkable. The excessive sugar intake began to subside, allowing the Pancreas to gradually recover from its strike. With renewed vigour, it started producing Insulin once again, restoring the delicate balance of sugar regulation in the town.

As the townspeople reduced their sugar intake, the cells of Bodyville began to experience a remarkable transformation. Glucose, the essential fuel for cellular energy, was now provided in controlled amounts. The cells rejoiced, eagerly absorbing the glucose and converting it into the energy they needed to thrive.

Simultaneously, the excess fat that had accumulated in the Adipose Tissue, the Fat Storage Facility, began to be utilized. The townspeople witnessed their waistlines shrinking and their bodies becoming leaner and healthier.

Among the key players in this journey was the liver, personified as a diligent worker. The liver had the vital task of processing excess sugar and converting it into usable energy or storing it as glycogen for future use. With the reduction in sugar consumption, the liver workload lightened, allowing it to perform its functions more efficiently.

The liver took on an additional role in the transformation process. It became responsible for metabolizing LDL-Cholesterol, which had been unfairly blamed for health issues. The townspeople learned that LDL-Cholesterol was not inherently bad but played a crucial role in transporting cholesterol throughout the body. It was the imbalanced sugar consumption that disrupted cholesterol metabolism and led to unfavourable health outcomes.

With this newfound understanding, the townspeople banished the misconceptions surrounding LDL-Cholesterol. They embraced a holistic approach to cholesterol management, focusing on maintaining a balanced diet, engaging in regular exercise, and incorporating foods rich in fibre, healthy fats, and antioxidants.

As the journey progressed, the townspeople witnessed a remarkable improvement in their overall well-being. Diabetes, the symbol of disrupted sugar regulation, slowly retreated as blood sugar levels stabilized within the healthy range. Obesity, inflammation, and fatigue syndrome also diminished, making way for a renewed sense of vitality and wellness.

Even Moody, the character symbolizing mood swings, began to fade away. The stabilization of blood sugar levels brought about emotional stability and a sense of inner calm for the townspeople.

In the midst of this transformation, the Pancreas regained its rightful place as the guardian of sugar.

Chapter 7

Gut Microbes, Love these Little Guys!

The gut microbiome is a community of tiny living organisms in our digestive system that helps keep us healthy. Two essential types of foods that support our gut health are prebiotics and probiotics.

Prebiotic Foods are like special fuel for the good bacteria in our gut. They help these good bacteria grow and stay active. Many prebiotic-rich foods are plant-based. They include a variety of fruits, vegetables, whole grains, and legumes. These plant foods are excellent sources of prebiotic fibres that nourish the beneficial bacteria in our gut and contribute to a healthy and diverse gut microbiome. Including a wide range of plant foods in our diet can

 help support gut health and overall well-being.

Probiotic Foods are like friendly soldiers that live in our gut and help fight off bad bacteria. They are live bacteria that are good for us. Yogurt, kefir, sauerkraut, and miso are examples of probiotic foods.

Eating a mix of these foods is essential because it promotes a diverse and healthy gut microbiome. A balanced gut helps us digest food better, strengthens our immune system, and may reduce the risk of some diseases.

Professor Tim Spector, a prominent researcher in the field of gut microbiome, has conducted extensive studies on the trillions of microorganisms residing in our digestive system, commonly known as gut microbes. Here are some key insights from his research:

Gut Microbe Diversity: The gut houses a diverse array of microbes, including bacteria, viruses, and fungi. This diversity significantly impacts gut health and supports various bodily functions.

Gut-Brain Interaction: The gut is often referred to as the "second brain" due to its bidirectional communication with the central nervous system. The gut microbiome influences brain function, mood, and behavior through the gut-brain axis.

Diet's Impact: Diet plays a pivotal role in shaping the composition of gut microbes. A varied and fiber-rich diet fosters a diverse and healthy gut microbiome, whereas a diet high in processed foods and sugars can negatively affect gut health.

Personalized Microbiome: Each individual possesses a unique gut microbiome influenced by factors like genetics, early life experiences, and environmental exposures. Understanding this personal aspect is vital for enhancing gut health.

Gut Microbes and Well-Being: The gut microbiome has been linked to various aspects of health, including immune function, metabolism, weight management, and the risk of certain diseases.

Antibiotics' Impact: Although antibiotics can be life-saving, they can also disrupt the balance of gut microbes. Proper use and consideration of probiotics after antibiotic treatment can help restore gut health.

Prebiotics and Probiotics: Prebiotics, dietary fibers nourishing beneficial gut microbes, and probiotics, live microorganisms conferring health benefits, play essential roles in gut health.

Gut Microbes and Chronic Conditions: Emerging research suggests that imbalances in the gut microbiome might contribute to the development of chronic diseases like obesity, diabetes, and inflammatory conditions.

Gut Microbes and Allergies: The gut microbiome plays a role in modulating the immune system's response, which may influence the development of allergies and autoimmune conditions.

Gut Microbe Diversity and Longevity: Some studies indicate that a diverse gut microbiome may correlate with better health and longevity.

Understanding the intricate and dynamic world of gut microbes presents an exciting frontier in health research. Nurturing a healthy gut microbiome through a balanced diet, regular exercise, and stress management is vital for overall well-being and holds the promise of personalized medicine's potential in the future.

Including prebiotic and probiotic-rich foods in our diet can be as simple as adding a banana to our breakfast or enjoying a cup of yogurt as a snack. Making these small changes can have a big impact on our overall health!

Prebiotic Foods:

Fruit

Garlic

Onions

Legumes, chickpeas, beans, kidney beans…

Asparagus, broccoli, cauliflower, and other yummy veggies

Jerusalem artichokes

Chicory root

Dandelion greens

Leeks

Apples, pears and other yummy fruits such as berries

seeds, nuts…

Cocoa

Seaweed

Probiotic Foods:

Yogurt (with live cultures) Full fat Greek

Kefir

Sauerkraut

Kimchi

Miso

Tempeh

Natto

Buttermilk (traditional)

Lassi

Kvass (fermented beetroot drink)

Traditional sourdough bread (made with natural fermentation)

Cheese (some varieties contain live probiotic cultures)

Pickles (fermented cucumbers, capers, olives)

Including a mix of these prebiotic and probiotic-rich foods in your diet can help promote a healthy gut and overall well-being. Remember that individual tolerance to certain foods may vary, so it's essential to listen to your body and make choices that best suit your health needs.

Amelia

Once upon a time, in a distant realm known as Harmonyville, there lived a determined young woman named Amelia. Harmonyville was a land where people cherished the balance between mind, body, and spirit. But one day, a formidable threat called "Cancer" emerged, casting a dark shadow over the once harmonious kingdom.

Amelia's grandfather, a wise herbalist, revealed a hidden secret to her. He explained that Cancer thrived on the excessive consumption of sugar and unhealthy eating habits prevalent in Harmonyville. The cancer cells fed on the sugary delights and processed foods, causing them to multiply uncontrollably.

Armed with this knowledge, Amelia embarked on a quest to find a way to defeat Cancer and restore balance to her beloved kingdom. She sought guidance from the realm's wise healers and scholars, who shared their insights on the power of nutrition and fasting in fighting cancer.

Amelia learned that reducing sugar intake and adopting a healthy, low-sugar diet could starve the cancer cells, weakening their ability to grow. She also discovered the wonders of fasting, a practice that lowered insulin levels, making it difficult for cancer cells to thrive.

With unwavering determination, Amelia returned to Harmonyville, determined to share her newfound knowledge with her fellow citizens. She started a movement encouraging everyone to make healthier food choices, cutting back on sugary treats and embracing nourishing, whole foods.

To demonstrate the benefits of fasting, Amelia organized community fasting days, where the people voluntarily refrained from eating for specific periods. These fasting days became a symbol of unity and strength, as the people of Harmonyville joined forces to combat Cancer.

As days turned into weeks, the kingdom witnessed a remarkable transformation. The once relentless growth of Cancer cells began to slow down. The people felt empowered and more in control of their health as they nourished their bodies with wholesome foods and embraced mindful eating.

Amelia's efforts did not go unnoticed. Her story inspired people far and wide, reaching neighbouring realms who sought her guidance in their battles against similar threats.

Amelia became known as the "Guardian of Health" for her courage and wisdom.

With time, Harmonyville regained its harmony, and Cancer's influence waned. The kingdom rejoiced, celebrating a newfound era of well-being and unity. Amelia's legacy lived on, and her teachings became an essential part of the realm's education, ensuring that future generations would be equipped with the knowledge to protect their health and maintain the delicate balance of Harmonyville.

And so, the tale of Amelia, the Guardian of Health, was etched into the annals of Harmonyville's history, a testament to the power of knowledge, mindful eating, and the determination to conquer adversity with courage and grace.

Catherine's Favourite Gut Microbe Breakfast Bowl

In a bowl...

Tablespoon of Full fat Greek Yogurt

Good Glug or Kefir

Handful of mixed nuts

Handful of mixed seeds

Handful of blueberries

Dessert spoon of chia Seeds

2 squares of broken pieces of 90% dark chocolate

Chapter 8

Proteins and Fats

Animal-based Proteins:

Chicken breast

Turkey

Eggs

Salmon

Greek yogurt

Plant-based Proteins:

Tofu

Lentils

Chickpeas

Black beans

Almonds

Quinoa

Saturated Fats:

Butter

Cheese

Fatty cuts of beef or pork

Coconut oil

Monounsaturated Fats:

Olive oil

Avocado

Nuts (e.g., almonds, peanuts, cashews)

Polyunsaturated Fats:

Fatty fish (e.g., salmon, mackerel, trout)

Flaxseeds

Chia seeds

Walnuts

Trans Fats (Avoid these):

Processed foods (e.g., cookies, cakes, pastries) made with partially hydrogenated oils.

It's important to remember that a healthy diet is about balance and moderation. Including a variety of whole, nutrient-dense foods from each macronutrient group can help ensure you're getting the essential nutrients your body needs to thrive.

Margarine is considered a trans-fat because of its production process. Trans fats are created when liquid vegetable oils undergo a process called hydrogenation, which involves adding hydrogen atoms to the oil's unsaturated fats. This process turns the liquid oil into a more solid and stable form, making it suitable for use in spreads like margarine and for commercial baking.

The hydrogenation process creates a specific type of fat called trans-fat, which has a unique molecular structure. Unlike natural fats found in foods like butter or olive oil, trans-fats have a straighter, more rigid shape. This molecular structure makes trans fats more stable and less likely to spoil or go rancid compared to natural fats.

However, despite their stability and long shelf life, trans fats are detrimental to our health. When consumed in excessive amounts, trans fats can increase the level of low-density lipoprotein (LDL) cholesterol in the bloodstream, also known as "bad" cholesterol. High LDL cholesterol is associated with an increased risk of heart disease and other cardiovascular problems.

Additionally, trans fats interfere with the body's ability to utilize essential fatty acids and may contribute to inflammation and other health issues.

Regarding gut microbes, the human digestive system is not well-equipped to break down and metabolize trans fats efficiently. Natural fats are broken down and utilized by our body's enzymes and gut bacteria as part of the normal digestion process. However, due to the unnatural and rigid molecular structure of trans fats, our gut microbes struggle to break them down effectively.

As a result, trans fats can remain in the digestive tract for more extended periods, potentially leading to issues like gut inflammation and alterations in gut microbiome composition. Moreover, consuming large amounts of trans fats can negatively impact gut health and contribute to various digestive and metabolic disorders.

For these reasons, it is advisable to limit or avoid the consumption of trans fats in your diet. Instead, opt for healthier fat sources, such as monounsaturated and polyunsaturated fats found in nuts, seeds, avocados, and fatty fish, to support your overall health and well-being.

Chapter 9

What Happens when we Cut out Sugar for two Weeks?

When you cut out refined sugar, ultra-processed foods, and sweetened foods and focus on consuming more natural, whole foods, you may experience various positive health changes. Here are 20 examples of potential improvements in health:

Improved Blood Sugar Control: Cutting out refined sugar helps stabilize blood sugar levels and reduce the risk of insulin resistance.

Reduced Inflammation: A whole-foods diet can help decrease chronic inflammation in the body.

Enhanced Digestion: A diet rich in natural foods may improve digestion and reduce gastrointestinal discomfort.

Better Skin Health: Fewer sugar spikes may lead to clearer skin and reduced acne.

Increased Energy Levels: Stable blood sugar levels can result in sustained energy throughout the day.

Better Mood: Balanced blood sugar levels can lead to improved mood and mental well-being.

Enhanced Concentration: Improved focus and concentration due to a stable supply of energy to the brain.

Reduced Risk of Chronic Diseases: A healthy diet can lower the risk of developing chronic conditions like type 2 diabetes, heart disease, and certain cancers.

Improved Heart Health: Lowering processed and sugary food intake can positively impact heart health by reducing cholesterol levels and blood pressure.

Enhanced Sleep Quality: A balanced diet may lead to improved sleep patterns and better rest.

Strengthened Immune System: Nutrient-dense foods support a robust immune system.

Balanced Hormones: Cutting out sugary foods can help balance hormones, leading to better overall hormonal health.

Improved Liver Function: A reduced sugar intake can support the liver in processing toxins more effectively.

Reduced Risk of Fatty Liver Disease: Eliminating excessive sugar can reduce the risk of non-alcoholic fatty liver disease.

Better Dental Health: Lower sugar intake can lead to improved oral health and reduced risk of cavities.

Increased Nutrient Intake: Whole foods are rich in essential vitamins, minerals, and antioxidants, supporting overall nutrition.

Improved Gut Health: A diet based on natural foods can promote a diverse and healthy gut microbiome.

Balanced Appetite: A whole-foods diet can help regulate appetite and reduce cravings for unhealthy foods.

Weight Loss: Eliminating sugary and processed foods can lead to gradual and sustainable weight loss.

Overall Sense of Well-Being: Improved physical health and balanced nutrition contribute to a greater sense of overall well-being and vitality.

When you cut back on or eliminate sugar from your diet, you may experience a decrease in cravings for sugary foods due to several physiological and psychological factors:

Reduced Reward System Activation: Sugar activates the brain's reward system, releasing dopamine—a "feel-good" neurotransmitter. Over time, this can create a reward-seeking cycle, leading to cravings for more sugary foods. When you reduce sugar intake, the brain's reward system may reset, and the cravings diminish.

Changing Taste Preferences: Regularly consuming sugary foods can alter your taste preferences, making you crave sweeter foods. By reducing sugar intake, your taste buds can adjust, and you may find yourself craving healthier, less sweet foods instead.

Increased Satiety: Sugary foods are often low in fibre and protein, which are essential for promoting feelings of fullness. When you eat more whole, nutrient-dense foods, you stay satiated for longer periods, reducing the desire for sugary snacks.

Breaking Habitual Patterns: Cravings for sugary foods can also be influenced by habits and emotional associations. By consciously avoiding sugary foods, you can break the habit of reaching for them in certain situations or emotional states.

Hormonal Regulation: Hormones like insulin and ghrelin play a role in hunger and satiety cues. Lowering sugar intake can help regulate these hormones, reducing cravings.

Mental and Emotional Benefits: Eliminating sugar can lead to better mental clarity and emotional stability, reducing emotional eating triggers and cravings.

It's important to note that initially, you may experience some withdrawal symptoms, such as irritability or headaches, as your body adjusts to the reduced sugar intake. However, as you persist in cutting back on sugar, the cravings typically subside, and you may find that you no longer feel as dependent on sugary foods to satisfy your appetite or emotions.

To support the process of reducing sugar cravings, focus on eating a balanced diet with a variety of whole foods, including fruits, vegetables, lean proteins, and healthy fats. Stay hydrated, get enough sleep, and manage stress effectively, as these factors can also influence sugar cravings. Always listen to your body's needs and consult with a healthcare professional or registered dietitian if you have specific health concerns or dietary goals.

Tip!

"Sugar's Deceptive Toll: Redefining Success Beyond Diets.

Acknowledging sugar's harm prompts a shift from quick-fix diets toward embracing a comprehensive lifestyle approach."

Chapter 11

Water

When we engage in physical activities, our bodies lose fluids and important minerals called electrolytes through sweat. Electrolytes are essential minerals that carry an electric charge in the body. They play a crucial role in various physiological processes and are vital for maintaining proper hydration, nerve function, muscle contractions, and pH balance. The major electrolytes in our body include sodium, potassium, calcium, magnesium, and chloride.

Hypotonic Drinks: These drinks have a lower concentration of solutes (like sugars and electrolytes) compared to our body's natural fluids. They quickly enter our bloodstream, making them great for rehydration during light activities or everyday life. However, they lack sufficient electrolytes to support intense workouts. Despite this, hypotonic drinks are excellent choices for staying hydrated during normal daily activities.

Isotonic Drinks: These drinks have a similar concentration of solutes to our body's fluids, allowing for rapid absorption and replenishment of fluids and electrolytes. Isotonic drinks are suitable for rehydration during moderate exercise or when you need to replenish fluids and electrolytes quickly. Popular isotonic sports drinks like Gatorade and Powerade provide hydration and essential electrolytes for athletes during moderate to intense workouts.

Hypertonic Drinks: These drinks have a higher concentration of solutes than our body's fluids. While they are not ideal for rehydration during exercise, they can be helpful after intense workouts to replenish glycogen stores and provide energy for recovery. An example of a hypertonic drink is chocolate milk, which contains higher levels of sugars and nutrients, making it suitable for post-workout recovery and refuelling.

Choosing Wisely:

For everyday hydration or light activities, stick to hypotonic drinks like water. They'll keep you well-hydrated without extra calories or sugars.

When engaging in moderate exercise or sports, isotonic drinks like Gatorade can help replace lost fluids and electrolytes.

Save hypertonic drinks for post-workout recovery, as they provide extra nutrients and energy.

Electrolytes are crucial for maintaining proper bodily functions during physical activities. Sports drinks are specifically designed to replenish these essential minerals along with fluids. However, not all situations require sports drinks. For most people, water and a balanced diet are sufficient to maintain electrolyte levels during normal daily activities.

It's essential to be savvy about our drink choices and opt for electrolyte-rich options when needed, such as during vigorous exercise, prolonged physical activity, or exposure to hot weather. In these situations, sports drinks can help prevent dehydration and maintain electrolyte balance.

While some sports drinks on the market can be helpful in replenishing electrolytes, others may contain high levels of added sugars and artificial ingredients, which can be harmful to health if consumed regularly. As savvy consumers, it's crucial to read the labels and choose wisely. Look for drinks with a balanced amount of electrolytes, minimal added sugars, and avoid those with artificial sweeteners and excessive preservatives.

For those who prefer a natural approach, making your own healthier electrolyte drinks at home is simple and cost-effective. You can create your isotonic beverage using natural ingredients like coconut water (rich in potassium and magnesium), adding a pinch of sea salt, and a splash of fresh lemon or lime juice to water. These homemade options provide a more natural and hydrating alternative to commercial sports drinks.

In conclusion, staying properly hydrated and maintaining electrolyte balance are essential for overall health and performance. By being informed and making conscious drink choices, you can ensure that you are giving your body the support it needs to function optimally and enjoy a healthy and active lifestyle. Always consider individual needs and opt for healthier alternatives, when possible, to promote long-term well-being.

Chapter 12
Watch out Hidden Sugars About!

Becoming sugar-savvy and making informed food choices starts with reading and understanding the information on food labels. Here's some advice on how to read the packets of foods and be more aware of hidden sugars:

Check the Ingredients List: Look for sugar and its various forms (e.g., sucrose, high fructose corn syrup, dextrose) in the ingredients list. Ingredients are listed in descending order by weight, so if sugar is one of the first few ingredients, it indicates a higher sugar content.

Look for Hidden Sugars: Be aware of sugar aliases and syrups like malt syrup, agave nectar, and brown rice syrup, which can disguise added sugars.

Check the Total Sugar Content: On the nutrition label, find the "Total Sugars" section. Keep in mind that natural sugars present in fruits or dairy products are different from added sugars. Focus on limiting added sugars.

Watch for Sugar-Free Claims: Foods labelled "sugar-free" may contain artificial sweeteners, which could still impact your health and sugar cravings. Read the ingredients list to confirm.

Consider the Serving Size: Pay attention to the serving size when assessing sugar content. Sometimes, the listed sugar content may apply to a smaller serving than what you typically consume.

Look for Whole Foods: Choose whole foods with minimal or no packaging, like fresh fruits, vegetables, lean meats, and whole grains. These foods are typically low in added sugars.

Compare Brands: Compare different brands of the same product to find options with lower sugar content. Some brands offer reduced-sugar or no-added-sugar versions.

Be Mindful of Processed Foods: Processed foods often contain hidden sugars to enhance flavour. opt for minimally processed or homemade alternatives when possible.

Use Apps and Online Resources: Some apps and websites allow you to scan barcodes and get detailed information about a product's nutritional content, including sugar.

Know Your Sugar Limits: Be aware of recommended daily sugar intake guidelines and aim to stay within those limits.

By developing the habit of reading food labels, you can make more conscious choices and become a sugar-savvy shopper, leading to a healthier and more balanced diet.

Being part of The Sugar Savvy Squad means that our focus goes beyond just weight loss! We understand that health and well-being are not solely determined by the numbers on a scale. Instead, we encourage you to embrace a holistic approach to eating and nourishing your body, prioritizing overall wellness and vitality.

Here's why focusing solely on weight loss may not always lead to optimal health:

Nutrient Deficiency: When you solely focus on caloric reduction, you may inadvertently miss out on essential nutrients that your body needs to function optimally. A nutrient-deficient diet can lead to fatigue, weakened immunity, and various health issues.

Gut Microbiome: Your gut is home to trillions of microbes that play a crucial role in digestion, immunity, and overall health. Drastically altering your diet to achieve weight loss can disrupt the balance of these beneficial microbes, affecting digestion and immunity.

Energy and Mood: Proper nutrition can significantly impact your energy levels and mood. Relying on restrictive diets for weight loss can leave you feeling fatigued and irritable, affecting your overall quality of life.

Skin Health: What you eat directly influences the health of your skin. Nutrient-dense foods nourish your skin from within, giving you that natural, radiant glow.

Inflammation: Chronic inflammation is linked to various health issues, including heart disease and autoimmune conditions. A diet rich in processed and sugary foods can fuel inflammation in the body.

Hormone Balance: Proper nutrition is essential for hormonal balance, which impacts everything from menstrual cycles to menopause symptoms.

Reversing Diabetes: A well-balanced diet can play a pivotal role in managing and even reversing type 2 diabetes.

Menopause and Period Symptoms: Certain foods can exacerbate menopause and menstrual symptoms, while others can help alleviate discomfort and balance hormones.

By revamping your eating habits and becoming part of the Sugar Savvy Squad, you can take back control of your life and experience a multitude of benefits:

Improved mood and mental well-being

Better sleep and increased energy levels

Enhanced skin health and appearance

Reduced inflammation and risk of chronic diseases

Balanced hormones and improved menstrual health

Reversed or better-managed diabetes symptoms

Here's a pecking order of importance when it comes to revamping what you eat:

Prioritize Nutrient-Dense Foods: Focus on foods rich in vitamins, minerals, and antioxidants, such as fruits, vegetables, whole grains, nuts, seeds, and legumes.

Nourish with Healthy Fats: Incorporate sources of healthy fats, like avocados, olive oil, nuts, grass fed butter, organic eggs, seeds and wild caught fish for brain function and overall well-being.

Include Adequate Protein: Choose good quality local organic meat and plant-based proteins like beans, lentils, tofu, and quinoa to support muscle health and repair. When it comes to meat go for quality over quantity. Chat to your local butcher and find out where the meat is sourced. Remember whatever the animal eats, you eat!

Reduce Added Sugars: Limit processed and sugary foods that can negatively impact blood sugar levels and overall health.

Hydrate: Stay well-hydrated with water, herbal teas, and natural beverages to support digestion and overall vitality.

Remember, being part of the Sugar Savvy Squad is about nourishing your body, mind, and soul with wholesome foods to achieve true well-being and vitality. Let's embark on this journey together and embrace a healthier, happier lifestyle!

Chapter 13

Antioxidants and Free Radicals

Many of us are told to eat fruits rich in antioxidants, but do we know why?

Free Radicals: Free radicals are highly reactive and unstable molecules that contain unpaired electrons. Due to this unpaired electron, they seek to stabilize themselves by stealing electrons from other molecules in the body. In the process, they can cause damage to these molecules, including important cellular components like DNA, proteins, and lipids. This damage is known as oxidative stress and can lead to various health issues, including inflammation, cell damage, and diseases like cancer and heart disease.

Antioxidants: Antioxidants are molecules that have the ability to neutralize free radicals by donating an electron without becoming unstable themselves. They act as defenders in the body, helping to protect cells from the harmful effects of free radicals. Antioxidants can be naturally produced by the body, but they can also be obtained from certain foods, particularly colourful fruits and vegetables. Common antioxidants include vitamins such as vitamin C and vitamin E, as well as minerals like selenium.

The balance between free radicals and antioxidants is essential for maintaining optimal health. When there is an excess of free radicals and insufficient antioxidants to neutralize them, oxidative stress can occur, leading to cellular damage and potential health problems. Consuming a diet rich in antioxidants helps support the body's defence system and reduces the risk of oxidative stress-related damage.

In summary, free radicals are reactive and unstable molecules that can cause damage to our cells, while antioxidants are protective molecules that help neutralize free radicals and maintain the balance in our bodies. By ensuring an adequate intake of antioxidants through a varied and colourful diet, we can help protect our cells and promote overall well-being.

TIP!

"Empower Your Plate: Embracing Health Beyond Weight Loss.

Nutritional knowledge empowers choices, enabling a focus on holistic health and well-being beyond simply losing weight."

Chapter 14

Popular Protein

Once upon a time in a colourful village called Nourish-Place, there lived three little friends – Milo the Muscle, Lily the Liver, and Kevin the Kidney. They were always eager to learn and explore the world of nutrition and health.

One sunny morning, as they gathered under the big apple tree, their wise teacher, Prof. NutriWisdom, told them about the wonders and challenges of protein. He explained that protein was like the building blocks for strong muscles, and it helped their bodies stay healthy and happy.

"But be careful, my little friends," warned Prof. NutriWisdom, "Too much protein can be tricky, especially for those with low muscle mass and liver and kidney problems."

Curious, Milo, Lily, and Kevin asked why. Prof. NutriWisdom smiled and began a tale of the adventures of protein in the body.

"Once upon a time," began Prof. NutriWisdom, "there was a grand feast in Nourish-Place with delicious protein-rich foods like nuts, beans, and fish. All the villagers were excited to try these tasty treats!"

"But some of the villagers, including our three friends, Milo, Lily, and Kevin, had special needs," continued Prof. NutriWisdom . "Milo wished to grow stronger muscles, but he learned that just eating lots of protein wouldn't magically make his muscles bigger."

Lily, the wise liver, chimed in, "Yes, and I am responsible for handling the protein in the body. If there's too much protein, I might have a hard time breaking it down, leading to trouble!"

Kevin, the thoughtful kidney, added, "And I must filter out waste products from the blood. If there's too much protein, I might get overwhelmed and struggle to keep everything in balance."

The three little friends listened intently, understanding the importance of balance. They decided to be mindful of their protein intake and seek guidance from the wise Prof. NutriWisdom, whenever they had questions.

So, whenever Milo, Lily, or Kevin felt like they needed more protein, they would visit Prof. NutriWisdom, who would carefully guide them. He suggested they eat a variety of healthy foods, like colourful fruits and vegetables, to get all the nutrients they needed.

The little friends also learned about the dangers of processed protein snacks, filled with added sugars and artificial ingredients. They decided to enjoy whole, unprocessed foods instead, which made them feel stronger and happier.

As time went by, Milo grew stronger, Lily's liver danced with joy, and Kevin's kidney function improved. They had become the healthiest and happiest trio in all of Nourish-Place!

And so, the little friends lived happily ever after, making smart choices about their protein intake, and sharing their newfound knowledge with all the villagers of Nourish-Place. And they all lived healthily and happily, ever after. The End.

"For individuals with kidney and liver problems and lack of muscle mass, managing protein intake is essential to safeguard their health. Seeking guidance from healthcare professionals like nutritionists or dietitians is crucial in determining the right amount of protein that meets their specific health needs without overburdening their organs.

But protein is just one part of the puzzle! To truly thrive, it's vital to maintain a balanced diet filled with a variety of nutrients. A balanced diet offers a wealth of benefits, including improved energy levels, better digestion, and enhanced overall well-being.

A balanced diet should include:

Colourful Fruits and Vegetables: These provide essential vitamins, minerals, and antioxidants that support the immune system and help combat illness.

Whole Grains: Rich in fibre and complex carbohydrates, whole grains provide sustained energy and aid in digestion.

Healthy Fats: Incorporating sources like avocados, nuts, and olive oil can support heart health and brain function.

Lean Proteins: Alongside plant-based proteins, lean sources of protein like poultry, fish, and legumes can provide the necessary building blocks for muscle repair and growth.

Water: Staying well-hydrated is crucial for bodily functions and overall health.

To ensure a balanced diet, one can focus on preparing more natural home-cooked meals. Home-cooked meals allow for greater control over ingredient choices, portion sizes, and cooking methods. This reduces reliance on ultra-processed and pre-packaged foods, which often contain excessive additives, salt, and unhealthy fats.

It's also important to avoid getting caught up in dietary dogma or restrictive eating patterns that may lead to nutrient deficiencies. Instead, embracing a flexible approach to eating and listening to one's body's cues can foster a healthy relationship with food.

For personalized guidance, individuals can invest in their health by booking an appointment with a registered nutritionist. A nutritionist can assess individual health needs, preferences, and lifestyle, tailoring dietary recommendations to optimize overall well-being.

Remember, making informed choices about our diets and nourishing our bodies with balanced, wholesome foods can lead to a healthier, happier life. So, let's savour the flavours of nutritious meals and embark on a journey to wellness together!"-Catherine

TIP!

"Put Wellness Over weight: Breaking Free from the Scale's Hold"

Focusing on well-being acknowledges complex factors, including sugar's influence on overall health beyond the scale."

PART 2

Chapter 15

Let's Begin!
Sugar Free Fortnight

The week leading up to Sugar-Free Fortnight is the perfect time to get prepared and set yourself up for success. As you embark on this journey to reset your taste buds and break free from the reliance on refined carbs and sugary foods, here's a comprehensive list to help you shop wisely and fill your cupboards with nourishing alternatives:

Load up on Fresh Produce: Stock up on a variety of fresh fruits and vegetables to satisfy your nutritional needs and provide natural sweetness without added sugars.

Healthy Fats: opt for sources of healthy fats like avocados, nuts, seeds, and olive oil to keep you satiated and support overall well-being.

Protein Power: Ensure your shopping list includes lean proteins like chicken, turkey, fish, tofu, and legumes to support muscle health and keep you feeling full.

Whole Grains: Swap out refined grains for wholesome options like quinoa, brown rice, oats, and spelt and rye products to maintain energy levels and support digestion.

Dairy Alternatives: Choose unsweetened plant-based milk and yogurt options to replace sugary dairy products and support your sugar-free journey.

Herbs and Spices: Enhance the flavour of your meals with an assortment of herbs and spices, such as cinnamon, vanilla, ginger, and nutmeg, without relying on added sugars.

Water and Herbal Teas: Stay hydrated with plenty of water and enjoy herbal teas without added sugars as refreshing and satisfying beverage options.

Read Labels Carefully: When choosing packaged foods, read labels diligently to avoid hidden sugars and processed ingredients.

Meal Prep: Plan your meals ahead of time to ensure you have nourishing and sugar-free options readily available, making it easier to resist sugary temptations.

Mindful Snacking: Keep sugar-free snacks like cut-up veggies, nuts, and homemade granola bars on hand for those moments when hunger strikes between meals.

Remember, Sugar-Free Fortnight is not about substituting sugary treats with artificial sweeteners or sugar-free alternatives that taste sweet. Instead, focus on embracing the natural flavours of whole foods and exploring new tastes and textures. The book offers valuable shopping tips, recipes, and support to guide you through this transformative journey towards a healthier relationship with food and a sugar-free lifestyle. By staying committed and mindful throughout the fortnight, you can achieve your wellness goals and experience the benefits of breaking free from the sweet taste and reliance on refined carbs.

Sugar-Free Fortnight is a transformative two-week program that challenges participants to eliminate sugar, refined carbs, and ultra-processed foods from their diets. By wiping the slate clean, the program aims to reset taste buds, reduce sugar cravings, and foster mindful eating habits. Participants embark on a journey of improved health, balanced blood sugar levels, and enhanced well-being. As part of the Sugar Savvy Squad community, members support and inspire each other throughout the fortnight, laying the foundation for a healthier and more empowered lifestyle.

Embarking on a sugar-free fortnight as the first action of being part of the Sugar Savvy Squad can be a transformative experience for your health and well-being.

By wiping the slate clean and cutting out sugar, refined carbs, and ultra-processed foods, you are giving your taste buds a chance to reset, reducing cravings for sweet treats.

Breaking the cycle of sugar dependency during this fortnight can help you make healthier choices and overcome emotional eating patterns.

By balancing blood sugar levels, you'll experience more consistent energy throughout the day and improve your mood.

Focusing on whole, nutrient-dense foods will provide your body with essential vitamins, minerals, and antioxidants, nourishing your cells and supporting overall health.

Reducing inflammation by eliminating inflammatory foods can lead to a sense of renewal and well-being.

Embracing mindful eating during this period will make you more aware of your food choices and promote a positive relationship with food.

Proper hydration during the sugar-free fortnight will support your body's natural detoxification processes.

With a clean slate, your body can heal and reload with new nutrients, paving the way for improved health and vitality.

As part of the Sugar Savvy Squad, you'll join a community of like-minded individuals, sharing support, tips, and recipes for a sugar-free lifestyle.

Completing the sugar-free fortnight successfully will boost your confidence in making long-term changes to your diet and lifestyle.

You'll discover the joy of natural flavours and find satisfaction in nourishing foods that support your well-being.

During this fortnight, you'll notice reduced sugar cravings, making it easier to maintain a healthier diet in the future.

The sugar-free fortnight is the first step towards building a strong foundation for a sustainable and healthy lifestyle.

By eliminating processed and sugary foods, you'll give your body a chance to rest and recharge, improving overall digestion.

As part of the Sugar Savvy Squad, you'll gain access to valuable resources and knowledge to support your journey towards better health.

The sugar-free fortnight will help you develop a more conscious approach to eating, making thoughtful food choices a habit.

You'll feel a sense of empowerment and pride in taking charge of your health and making positive changes.

After the sugar-free fortnight, you'll have a greater appreciation for the impact of sugar on your health and be better equipped to make informed choices for a healthier, happier life.
The week before sugar Free Fortnight get prepared. You'll need to go shopping and fill your cupboards with
       Let's Start your Journey into Wellness!

Using this table, you can record your daily meals and snacks in the Breakfast, Lunch, and Dinner columns. Additionally, rate your mood and pain level on the respective scales and note any observations about your sleep each day. This food diary and observation log will help you track your progress throughout the first week of your Sugar Savvy Squad journey and identify any patterns or changes that may need to be tweaked, which could help your

	Breakfast	Lunch	Dinner	Mood Happy Fair Low
Mon				
Tues				
Wed				
Thur				
Fri				

Sat				
Sun				

What time did do you eat your first meal of the day?

What time did you eat your last meal of the day?

How long did you go in between meals? I.e., needed to snack regularly, felt hungry every couple of hours, none of the above.

Would you say that your meal choices were mostly unprocessed/minimally processed, ultra processed?

Did you manage to incorporate a minimum of 30 different plants into your weekly diet?

Are you considering making some savvy swaps to improve your health? If so, where do you think you could implement changes? For example, cutting back on fizzy drinks, starting your day with a savoury option, incorporating more plant-based foods into your diet, adding more fibre to your meals to prevent snacking, and having an earlier evening meal may all be beneficial choices.

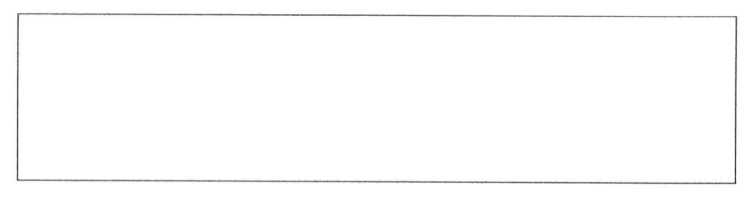

To help you through Sugar Free Fortnight!

Savvy Swaps

Refined carbohydrates, like white bread, pasta, and sugary cereals, can wreak havoc on the bloodstream due to their rapid digestion and absorption. When consumed, they cause a quick spike in blood sugar levels, leading to a surge of insulin production from the pancreas. This rollercoaster effect often leaves us feeling energized momentarily but quickly leads to a crash, leaving us tired and craving more sugary foods.

To make healthier swaps, consider opting for nutrient-rich alternatives that provide sustained energy and don't cause drastic blood sugar fluctuations. Instead of pasta, try zucchini noodles or cauliflower rice, which are lower in carbohydrates and higher in vitamins and minerals. Swap sugary cereals for whole-grain options with no added sugars and top them with fresh fruit for natural sweetness.

By making these simple changes, you can support stable blood sugar levels, improve energy levels, and reduce cravings, ultimately promoting better overall health and well-being.

Refined Carbohydrates:

bread

White rice

Regular pasta

Store-bought cookies

Pastries

Donuts

Cakes

Muffins

Pancakes and waffles made with white flour

White flour tortillas

Pretzels

Crackers

Bagels

Instant oatmeal with added sugar

Sugary cereals

Potato chips

Candy bars

Sugary breakfast bars

Soft drinks and soda

Fruit juices with added sugar

Ice cream

Sugary energy drinks

Flavoured yogurt with added sugars

Fruit-flavoured snacks, dried fruit, fruit roll ups…

Sugary canned fruits

White pizza crust

Sweetened iced tea

Sugary condiments (ketchup, BBQ sauce, etc.)

Honey-roasted nuts

Fruit preserves or jams with added sugars

Commercially sweetened smoothies

White sugar, brown sugar, and powdered sugar

Sweetened flavoured coffee drinks

Fruit-flavoured yogurt drinks

Instant pudding mixes

Sweetened canned soups

Bottled fruit and vegetable juices

Commercially prepared salad dressings with added sugars

Sweetened canned beans or baked beans

Sugary flavoured water

Sweetened iced coffee beverages.

Sugary sports drinks

Canned fruit pie fillings

Commercially sweetened nut milk

Flavoured granola, cereal and muesli

Sugary cocktail mixers

Marshmallows and marshmallow spreads

Fruit-flavoured gelatine desserts

Sweetened fruit sauces or syrups

Sugary dried fruits (e.g., candied fruits)

Condiments

TIP For Vegans and Vegetarians

During a sugar-free fortnight, it's important for vegans and vegetarians to consider their diet, especially regarding rice and whole grain foods. These individuals must ensure they're consuming all eight essential amino acids, which are vital for proteins. Unlike animal proteins, plant sources may lack some amino acids. By eating a variety of plant foods like beans, nuts, and seeds, they can combine these for all amino acids. Whole grains like rice are crucial too, complementing amino acids in legumes for a balanced protein intake. This ensures optimal nutrition for vegans and vegetarians during their sugar-free period.

Healthier Alternatives:

Rye bread or Spelte bread

Cauliflower rice or broccoli rice

Zucchini noodles or "zoodles"

Handfuls of mixed nuts, seeds and fresh berries to add to your breakfast bowl, opposed to shop bought granola or muesli

Fresh fruit salad with no added sugars

Cooled baked sweet potato wedges

Nut butter on apple slices or celery sticks

Greek yogurt with berries and a drizzle of honey

Dark chocolate-covered almonds or walnuts

Chia seed pudding with unsweetened or homemade almond milk

Full fat Greek yogurt

Baked vegetable chips (e.g., kale chips, beet chips)

Homemade energy bars with dates and nuts

Cucumber slices with hummus

Roasted chickpeas with spices

Frozen grapes or berries as a refreshing snack

Coconut chips or coconut flakes

Almond flour or coconut flour

Flaxseed crackers or chia seed crackers

Avocado chocolate mousse with no added sugars

Unsweetened nut milk (almond, cashew, coconut)

Roasted seaweed snacks

Edamame beans with sea salt

Fresh guacamole with vegetable sticks

Coconut water as a natural hydrating option

Apple and cheese

Quinoa as a nutritious grain alternative

Lentils or chickpea instead of pasta

Fresh fruit and nuts

Mixed nuts

Cooled sweet potato wedges

Unsweetened herbal teas or infused water

Unsweetened almond milk for beverages and cooking

Homemade fruit popsicles using natural fruit juice

Whole grain wraps or lettuce wraps for sandwiches

Homemade tomato sauce with no added sugars

Homemade Cottage cheese ice cream

Homemade vegetable soup with natural seasonings

Steamed or roasted vegetables with herbs and spices

Hummus

Homemade guacamole with fresh lime and cilantro

Nut and seed mix with no added sugars

Unsweetened coconut milk for cooking and baking

Baked chickpeas with a touch of olive oil and spices

Unsweetened coconut flakes as a topping for yogurt or smoothies

Cheese!

Fresh fruit kabobs

Baked cinnamon-spiced apple slices

Homemade hummus with lemon and garlic

Unsweetened almond butter or peanut butter

Vegetable chips made from beets, carrots, or sweet potatoes

Olives, Gherkins, Capers, pickled onions, sundried tomatoes and peppers in olive oil

These alternatives offer a wide variety of delicious and nutrient-dense options that can help you avoid refined carbs and added sugars while still enjoying a satisfying and healthful diet.

The Sugar Savvy Squad's
"Low Sugar Lifestyle List!"

1. Prioritize Vegetables, Protein, and Starches: Start your meals with a generous serving of vegetables, followed by lean protein and then starches. This structured eating approach helps regulate blood sugar levels and reduces sugar cravings.

2. Beware of Hidden Sugars in Processed Foods: Many processed foods like low-fat yogurts, cereals, granola, health bars, shakes, and smoothies contain hidden sugars. They may seem healthy but often have added sugars that can spike blood sugar levels. Always read labels and choose options with lower added sugar content.

3. Avoid Empty-Calorie Snacks: Cookies, baked goods, crisps, crackers, puff wheat snacks, and cheese straws

often lack satiety due to their low fiber and protein content. We tend to overeat them because they don't provide a feeling of fullness. Instead, opt for snacks with a balance of nutrients to keep you satisfied.

4. Individual Metabolism Matters: It's essential to remember that not everyone metabolizes calories in the same way. Factors like age, gender, genetics, muscle mass, and activity level influence how our bodies process and utilize calories. This means that calorie counting alone may not always be an accurate indicator of health or weight management.

5. Sugary Foods and Blood Sugar: Foods high in added sugars can lead to rapid spikes and crashes in blood sugar levels, which can contribute to energy fluctuations, cravings, and overeating. Reducing sugar intake helps maintain more stable energy levels.

6. Low-Fat Doesn't Always Mean Healthy: Low-fat products often compensate for reduced fat content by adding sugar to improve taste. This can make them less nutritious than their full-fat counterparts. Choose foods based on overall nutritional quality rather than just fat content.

7. Balance Your Macros: Prioritize meals and snacks that offer a balance of carbohydrates, protein, and healthy fats.

This combination promotes satiety, helps control blood sugar, and supports overall well-being.

8. Set a Cutoff Time for Evening Eating: Establish a specific time in the evening after which you avoid consuming calories. This practice allows your body to enter a prolonged overnight fast, promoting better digestion, improved metabolism, and potentially aiding in weight management.

9. Choose Whole Fruits over Fruit Juices: Whole fruits contain fiber, which slows down the absorption of sugar and helps regulate blood sugar levels. Fruit juices, on the other hand, often lack fiber and can lead to quick sugar spikes.

10. Learn to Read Labels: Develop the skill of reading food labels to identify hidden sugars. Look out for various terms like high fructose corn syrup, cane sugar, or sucrose, which indicate added sugars in products.

11. Opt for Natural Sweeteners Sparingly: While natural sweeteners like honey and maple syrup may seem healthier, they are still sources of sugar. Use them in moderation and be mindful of portion sizes.

12. Cook at Home: Preparing your meals at home gives you control over the ingredients and allows you to reduce sugar and unhealthy fats in your dishes.

13. Practice Moderation with Desserts: Occasional treats are okay, but try to limit consumption of sugary desserts, and savor them mindfully when you do indulge.

14. Stay Hydrated with Water: Sometimes thirst can be mistaken for hunger. Drinking water throughout the day can help reduce cravings for sugary beverages or snacks.

15. Experiment with Spices: Flavor your food with natural spices like cinnamon, vanilla, or nutmeg. These can add sweetness without added sugar.

16. Manage Stress: High stress levels can lead to emotional eating and cravings for sugary comfort foods. Practice stress-reduction techniques like meditation, yoga, or deep breathing.

17. Get Adequate Sleep: Lack of sleep can disrupt hunger hormones and increase cravings for sugary and high-calorie foods. Aim for 7-9 hours of quality sleep each night.

By incorporating these additional tips, including setting a cutoff time for evening eating, you can further enhance your sugar-savvy eating habits and promote overall health and well-being.

Starting the day off Right and Food Sequencing

Starting the day off with a savoury meal and prioritizing vegetables, proteins, and fats before carbohydrates can have various health benefits:

Stable Blood Sugar Levels: Eating vegetables first helps stabilize blood sugar levels. Vegetables are low in carbohydrates and high in fibre, which slows down the absorption of sugars into the bloodstream. This prevents rapid spikes and crashes in blood sugar levels, promoting sustained energy throughout the morning.

Nourishing Nutrients: Vegetables are rich in essential vitamins, minerals, and antioxidants, providing your body with a nourishing start to the day. Prioritizing vegetables ensures that you get a good dose of nutrients from the very beginning.

Satiety and Appetite Control: Starting with proteins and fats before carbohydrates can enhance feelings of satiety and control appetite. Proteins and fats are more filling and help you stay satisfied for longer, reducing the likelihood of overeating carbohydrates later in the day.

Improved Digestion: Eating vegetables first can also aid digestion. Fiber-rich vegetables help promote regular bowel movements and support a healthy gut environment.

Better Nutrient Absorption: Consuming proteins and fats before carbohydrates can optimize nutrient absorption. Certain nutrients, like fat-soluble vitamins (A, D, E, K), are better absorbed in the presence of dietary fats.

Balanced Energy: Prioritizing proteins and fats in the morning provides a balanced source of energy, avoiding the energy crashes that can occur after consuming high-carbohydrate meals.

Weight Management: This eating pattern can support weight management efforts by promoting satiety and reducing cravings for sugary or high-calorie foods.

It's important to note that individual preferences and dietary needs vary, and there is no one-size-fits-all approach to eating. However, this eating order is a practical guideline that many people find beneficial for maintaining stable energy levels, supporting overall health, and making mindful food choices throughout the day.

Ten Savoury Breakfast Ideas, for Egg Lovers

Here are ten savoury breakfast ideas that include eggs, vegetables, and a source of probiotics:

Veggie Omelette: Whisk eggs and fold in sautéed spinach, bell peppers, onions, and mushrooms. Top with a dollop of Greek yogurt for a probiotic boost.

Scrambled Eggs with Sautéed Greens: Scramble eggs and serve with a side of sautéed kale, Swiss chard, or spinach. Add a spoonful of kimchi or fermented vegetables for probiotics.

Breakfast Burrito Bowl: Prepare a bowl with scrambled eggs, black beans, avocado slices, and a generous serving of mixed greens. Top it off with a spoonful of yogurt-based dressing for probiotics.

Frittata with Roasted Vegetables: Make a frittata using eggs and roast a mix of your favourite vegetables like zucchini, tomatoes, and bell peppers. Serve with a side of probiotic-rich kefir or yogurt.

Shakshuka: Poach eggs in a tomato and bell pepper sauce with onions, garlic, and spices. Add a side of pickled vegetables or kimchi for probiotics.

Egg and Veggie Muffins: Make mini muffins with eggs, diced vegetables, and a sprinkle of feta cheese. Serve with a side of Greek yogurt mixed with fresh herbs for probiotics.

Quiche with Spinach and Mushrooms: Bake a crustless quiche with eggs, sautéed spinach, and mushrooms. Pair with a side of sauerkraut or fermented pickles for probiotics.

Breakfast Salad: Create a salad with mixed greens, hard-boiled eggs, cherry tomatoes, cucumbers, and avocado. Drizzle with a probiotic-rich buttermilk or yogurt dressing.

Egg and Vegetable Stir-Fry: Stir-fry eggs with a variety of colourful vegetables like broccoli, carrots, and snap peas. Serve alongside a small bowl of miso soup for probiotics.

Eggs Benedict with Sauteed Asparagus: Make a classic Eggs Benedict but substitute the English muffin with sautéed asparagus spears. Enjoy with a side of yogurt or kefir for probiotics.

Steak Breakfast Ideas

These steak-inspired breakfast ideas offer a protein-packed and delicious way for meat lovers to kickstart their day with a satisfying and nutritious meal.

Steak and Eggs Benedict: Replace the traditional ham in Eggs Benedict with slices of perfectly cooked steak. Top with poached eggs and hollandaise sauce.

Steak and Avocado Breakfast Salad: Combine sliced steak with fresh avocado, cherry tomatoes, mixed greens, and a sprinkle of feta cheese. Drizzle with a vinaigrette.

Steak and Vegetable Scramble: Sauté strips of steak with colourful bell peppers, onions, and spinach. Add scrambled eggs and cook until they are fluffy and fully cooked.

Steak Breakfast Tacos: Fill corn or lettuce taco shells with grilled steak, pico de gallo, and a dollop of guacamole or sour cream.

Steak and Sweet Potato Hash: Create a hearty hash by sautéing diced sweet potatoes and steak together with onions and bell peppers.

Steak and Egg Stuffed Portobello Mushrooms: Remove the stems from Portobello mushrooms, fill the caps with sliced steak and crack an egg on top. Bake until the eggs are cooked to your liking.

Steak and Cheese Omelette: Prepare a steak and cheese omelette by folding slices of cooked steak and shredded cheese into fluffy eggs.

Steak and Mushroom Breakfast Skillet: Cook steak with sliced mushrooms and garlic in a skillet. Add in scrambled eggs and cook until they are set.

Steak and Asparagus Breakfast Stir-Fry: Stir-fry sliced steak with asparagus and cherry tomatoes. Serve with scrambled eggs on top.

Catherine's favourite! Steak, fried mushrooms, wilted spinach and two fried eggs topped with blue cheese!

TIP!

"Holistic Health: Rethinking Goals Beyond Weight Loss

Prioritizing well-being over weight considers sugar's impact on energy levels and vitality, embracing a broader health perspective."

Greek Yogurt Breakfast Ideas:

Berry Nut Medley: Mix Greek yogurt with a variety of fresh berries (e.g., blueberries, raspberries, blackberries) and a handful of mixed nuts (e.g., almonds, walnuts, pistachios).

Greek Yogurt and Chia Seed Pudding: Combine Greek yogurt with chia seeds and refrigerate overnight. Top with sliced strawberries, kiwi, and a sprinkle of sunflower seeds.

Greek Yogurt Veggie Roll-Ups: Spread Greek yogurt on collard green leaves and add sliced cucumbers, bell peppers, and avocado. Roll them up for a nutritious and refreshing breakfast.

Greek Yogurt Protein Bowl: Mix Greek yogurt with a scoop of protein powder (e.g., whey or plant-based) and add a handful of mixed berries, crushed almonds, and flaxseeds.

Greek Yogurt Stuffed Peppers: Fill halved bell peppers with Greek yogurt and top with a mix of diced tomatoes, cucumbers, and olives for a savoury and satisfying breakfast.

Kefir Breakfast Ideas:

Kefir Chia Seed Smoothie: Blend kefir with frozen mixed berries, spinach, and a spoonful of almond butter. Top with a handful of sliced almonds and a few fresh blueberries.

Kefir and Mixed Nut Salad Dressing: Whisk kefir with lemon juice, Dijon mustard, and a pinch of salt and pepper. Drizzle over a mixed greens salad topped with toasted almonds and sesame seeds.

Kefir Avocado Boat: Fill halved avocados with kefir and top with a mix of diced strawberries, blackberries, and chopped pistachios.

Kefir Green Goddess Bowl: Blend kefir with spinach, parsley, and a splash of apple cider vinegar. Pour over a bowl of sliced cucumbers, cherry tomatoes, and pumpkin seeds.

Kefir Berry Smoothie Bowl: Blend kefir with frozen mixed berries and a dash of cinnamon. Pour into a bowl and top with sliced kiwi, shredded coconut, and hemp seeds.

These Greek yogurt and kefir breakfast ideas are packed with nutrients, probiotics, and a variety of delicious and

nourishing ingredients to help you start your day on a healthy and flavourful note.

Breaking fast is the most important meal of the day. If you feel hungry after your yogurt bowl, then eat something else on top such as boiled eggs, an avocado or nut butter with crudites. Remember tomorrow is another day, and a great opportunity to think about where we can make tweaks and adjustments.

A Message from Catherine

Breaking your fast is indeed a crucial meal that sets the tone for the day ahead. While a yogurt bowl can be a nutritious choice, it's essential to listen to your body's signals and respond accordingly. If you still feel hungry after your yogurt bowl, consider adding additional nourishing elements to ensure you start the day feeling satisfied and energized.

Adding protein-rich foods like boiled eggs can provide a longer-lasting feeling of fullness and support muscle repair and maintenance. Avocado, with its healthy fats and fibre, can also be a great addition, promoting satiety and supporting heart health. Alternatively, nut butter paired with colourful crudites offers a delightful mix of flavours and textures while providing essential nutrients and antioxidants.

Remember, everyone's nutritional needs and hunger levels vary, so it's okay to adapt your meals to suit your unique preferences and requirements. Embrace the flexibility that each new day brings, allowing yourself to explore and experiment with different combinations of foods to find what truly nourishes and satisfies you.

Moreover, this journey towards improved health and well-being is not about perfection but progress. It's about embracing the opportunities for growth and learning along the way. If you find yourself craving something sweet or indulging in a treat now and then, don't fret. Instead, use it as a chance to reflect on your overall dietary patterns and make mindful adjustments moving forward.

Each day is a fresh start, a chance to make positive tweaks to your diet and lifestyle. Whether it's opting for more vegetables at meals, drinking more water, or incorporating mindful eating practices, each small change can contribute to your overall health journey.

Remember, this is a process of self-discovery and empowerment. It's about nourishing your body and soul with choices that align with your well-being goals. Trust yourself and your body's wisdom to guide you on this path of transformation.

So, as you break your fast each morning, do so with gratitude for the nourishment it provides and with the excitement of creating a day filled with vitality and joy. Tomorrow brings endless opportunities for growth and the chance to further enhance your health journey.

With each new day, may you find the balance that fuels your body and soul, embracing the journey with a sense of curiosity, resilience, and self-compassion. As you continue to explore the world of nutrition and wellness, always remember that progress is the ultimate goal, and every step forward is a testament to your commitment to self-improvement.

So, go forth with confidence and joy, nourishing yourself from the inside out, and relishing in the beautiful symphony of flavours, colours, and textures that real, whole foods have to offer. You have the power to make a difference in your life, and each choice you make is a step towards a healthier, happier you.

With love and encouragement on this journey of transformation,

Catherine x

Plant Based Breakfast

How to make a plant based omelette

75g chickpea flour

120ml water

1 tablespoon nutritional yeast (optional, for a cheesy flavour)

1/4 teaspoon turmeric (for colour)

Pinch of black salt (kala namak) for an eggy taste (optional)

Salt and pepper to taste

25g diced vegetables (e.g., onions, bell peppers, tomatoes, spinach, mushrooms)

1 tablespoon cooking oil (e.g., olive oil, coconut oil)

Instructions:

In a mixing bowl, whisk together chickpea flour, water, nutritional yeast (if using), turmeric, black salt (if using), salt, and pepper until you get a smooth batter. Let it sit for a few minutes to thicken.

In a non-stick skillet or frying pan, heat the cooking oil over medium heat.

Add the diced vegetables to the pan and sauté them until they are slightly softened.

Pour the chickpea flour batter over the sautéed vegetables, spreading it out evenly to form a round shape like an omelette.

Cook the omelette on medium heat for about 3-4 minutes or until the edges start to lift and the bottom is golden brown.

Carefully flip the omelette using a spatula and cook the other side for an additional 2-3 minutes until cooked through.

Once the omelette is cooked to your liking, remove it from the pan and serve hot.

You can customize your vegan omelette with any of your favourite fillings, such as dairy-free cheese, vegan bacon or sausage, avocado, or any other vegetables you enjoy. It's a versatile and nutritious breakfast option that's completely plant-based and egg-free!

Here are ten plant-based, high-protein, low-sugar, and wheat-free breakfast ideas:

Chickpea Flour Pancakes: Make savoury pancakes using chickpea flour, chopped spinach, and diced bell peppers. Top with sliced avocado and a drizzle of tahini.

Tofu Scramble: Sauté crumbled tofu with diced tomatoes, onions, and your favourite spices (such as turmeric and cumin) for a hearty and protein-packed scramble.

Chia Seed Pudding: Create a chia seed pudding with almond milk, chia seeds, and a touch of vanilla extract. Top with fresh berries and sliced almonds.

Quinoa Breakfast Bowl: Cook quinoa and mix it with sliced banana, chopped nuts, and a dollop of almond or coconut yogurt.

Nut Butter Smoothie: Blend almond or peanut butter with frozen berries, spinach, and a splash of almond milk for a creamy and satisfying smoothie.

Lentil Breakfast Bowl: Prepare cooked lentils with roasted sweet potatoes, steamed broccoli, and a tahini-lemon dressing.

Sweet Potato Toast: Slice sweet potatoes and toast them until tender. Top with mashed avocado and sprinkle with pumpkin seeds.

Hemp Seed Yogurt Parfait: Layer coconut or almond yogurt with hemp seeds, shredded coconut, and fresh berries.

Spinach and Mushroom Vegan Omelette: Use chickpea flour as a base for a vegan omelette filled with sautéed spinach, mushrooms, and dairy-free cheese.

Banana Bread: Mash two large ripe bananas into a rounded tablespoon of peanut butter. Mix in 1 rounded dessert spoon of high percentage cocoa powder. Pop into a loaf tin for about 20 minutes at 160. You may need to stir in a teeny bit of maple syrup! Sprinkle with mixed nuts to bulk up the fibre and protein.

These plant-based breakfast ideas offer a variety of flavours, textures, and nutrients while being free of wheat and low in sugar. They are perfect for those looking for high-protein, nourishing breakfast options to fuel their day.

Here are seven low-sugar, high-protein, and fiber-rich lunch ideas that are free from starch:

Grilled Chicken Salad:

Grilled chicken breast served over a bed of mixed greens, cherry tomatoes, cucumbers, and avocado. Drizzle with a tangy vinaigrette made with olive oil and lemon juice.

Tuna and Avocado Wraps:

Mix canned tuna with mashed avocado, chopped celery, and red onions. Spread the mixture on large lettuce leaves and roll them up for a delicious and refreshing wrap.

Chickpea and Veggie Stir-Fry:

Sauté chopped bell peppers, broccoli, and snap peas in a little olive oil. Add cooked chickpeas and a splash of low-sodium soy sauce for a flavourful and satisfying stir-fry.

Zucchini Noodles with Pesto and Grilled Shrimp:

Spiralize zucchini to create "noodles" and top them with homemade basil pesto and grilled shrimp for a tasty and nutrient-packed dish.

Smoked Salmon and Cucumber Bites:

Top cucumber slices with a dollop of cream cheese or dairy-free alternative and a slice of smoked salmon. Garnish with fresh dill for an elegant and protein-rich lunch.

Turkey Lettuce Wraps:

Brown lean ground turkey with garlic, ginger, and a splash of low-sodium soy sauce. Serve the flavourful turkey mixture in large lettuce leaves for a light and satisfying meal.

Quinoa and Veggie Bowl:

Combine cooked quinoa with a variety of roasted or raw vegetables like cherry tomatoes, roasted bell peppers, shredded carrots, and edamame. Drizzle with a lemon-tahini dressing for added flavour.

These lunch ideas are not only low in sugar and starch but also packed with protein and fibre, providing a well-rounded and nutritious meal to keep you energized and satisfied throughout the day!

Chapter 16

Meal Prepping

Meal prepping lunches that are high in protein, low in sugar, and rich in fibre can be a fantastic way to ensure you have nutritious and satisfying meals ready to go throughout the week. Here are five delicious and easy meal prep lunch ideas to get you started: Ditch the meal deals and take back the control of what goes into your wonderful body.

Quinoa and Black Bean Salad:

Cook quinoa and mix it with black beans, diced bell peppers, cherry tomatoes, chopped cucumbers, and fresh cilantro. Dress it with a lime vinaigrette made with olive oil, lime juice, garlic, and a touch of honey or maple syrup (for a small amount of natural sweetness).

Grilled Chicken and Vegetable Skewers:

Thread chunks of grilled chicken breast and colourful veggies (like bell peppers, zucchini, and red onions) onto skewers. Serve with a side of hummus for dipping and a mixed green salad.

Tofu Stir-Fry with Broccoli and Snap Peas:

Stir-fry cubed tofu with garlic, ginger, broccoli florets, and snap peas in a sesame oil-based sauce (low-sodium soy sauce, sesame oil, rice vinegar). Serve it over cauliflower rice for an additional fibre boost.

Lentil and Vegetable Soup:

Prepare a hearty lentil and vegetable soup using a variety of colourful vegetables like carrots, celery, spinach, and bell peppers. Season with herbs and spices like thyme, oregano, and a bay leaf for added flavour.

Salmon and Asparagus Foil Packets:

Wrap salmon fillets and fresh asparagus spears in foil with a drizzle of olive oil and lemon juice. Bake the packets in the oven until the salmon is cooked through and the asparagus is tender. Serve with a side of quinoa or a green salad.

Remember to use herbs, spices, and natural flavour enhancers like lemon, lime, or vinegar to add taste without relying on added sugars. Meal prepping these high-protein, low-sugar, and fibre-rich lunches will not only save you time but also help you stay on track with your healthy eating goals. Enjoy your delicious and nutritious meals throughout the week!

Staying fresh and full of vitality during lunchtime is essential for maintaining energy levels and productivity throughout the day. Here are some tips to help you achieve just that:

Eat a Balanced Lunch: Include a combination of lean proteins (such as chicken, fish, tofu, or beans), healthy fats (like avocado, nuts, or olive oil), and fibre-rich vegetables or whole grains in your lunch. This balanced meal will keep you feeling satisfied and provide a steady release of energy.

Stay Hydrated: Drink plenty of water throughout the day to stay hydrated. Dehydration can lead to fatigue, so aim to have a glass of water with your lunch to maintain your energy levels.

Avoid Heavy, Greasy Foods: Heavy, greasy foods can leave you feeling sluggish and weighed down. Opt for lighter, nutrient-dense options to keep you feeling fresh and energized.

Incorporate Fresh Fruits and Vegetables: Include fresh fruits and vegetables in your lunch to boost your vitamin and mineral intake. They provide essential nutrients that help support your immune system and overall well-being.

Choose Low-Sugar Options: Avoid high-sugar foods and beverages that can lead to energy crashes later in the day. Opt for low-sugar or naturally sweetened alternatives to maintain stable blood sugar levels.

Take Short Walks: If possible, take a short walk during your lunch break to get some fresh air and stretch your legs. Physical activity can help boost your mood and energy levels.

Practice Mindful Eating: Eat your lunch mindfully, savouring each bite and paying attention to your body's hunger and fullness cues. This can prevent overeating and promote better digestion.

Pack Your Lunch: Preparing your lunch in advance allows you to control the ingredients and portion sizes. It also saves time and money, ensuring you have a nutritious and satisfying meal ready to go.

Limit Caffeine and Alcohol: While a cup of coffee may provide a temporary energy boost, excessive caffeine or alcohol consumption can lead to dehydration and disrupt your sleep patterns. Moderation is key.

Practice Stress-Reduction Techniques: Stress can drain your vitality, so take a few minutes during lunch to practice relaxation techniques like deep breathing, meditation, or gentle stretching.

By incorporating these tips into your lunchtime routine, you can maintain your vitality and feel fresh and energized for the rest of the day!

Why is ui important to add these hacks into your lunchtime living?

Boosts Energy: Physical activity increases blood flow and oxygen delivery to the muscles and brain, providing an instant boost of energy and alertness. This can help combat the midday slump and keep you feeling more focused and productive for the afternoon.

Relieves Stress: Exercise releases endorphins, which are natural mood boosters that reduce stress and anxiety. Taking a break from work and moving your body can help clear your mind, alleviate tension, and improve your overall well-being.

Enhances Mood: Physical activity triggers the release of neurotransmitters like dopamine and serotonin, which promote feelings of happiness and relaxation. Moving during lunch can help improve your mood and create a more positive outlook on the day.

Improves Concentration: Regular movement has been shown to enhance cognitive function and memory. Taking a short walk or engaging in light exercise can help you return to work with improved focus and mental clarity.

Supports Physical Health: Incorporating movement into your day can help you maintain a healthy weight, improve cardiovascular health, and reduce the risk of chronic diseases like diabetes and heart disease.

Aids Digestion: Light movement after eating can aid digestion by promoting gentle contractions of the muscles in the digestive tract. This can help prevent feelings of bloating or discomfort after a meal.

Encourages Social Interaction: Taking a walk or participating in a group fitness class during lunchtime can be an opportunity to socialize with colleagues or friends, fostering positive relationships and reducing feelings of isolation.

Provides Fresh Air and Nature Exposure: If possible, getting outdoors during lunchtime allows you to enjoy fresh air and connect with nature. Nature exposure has been linked to reduced stress and improved mental well-being.

Promotes a Healthy Work-Life Balance: Taking time for yourself during lunch to move and focus on your well-being can help create a healthier work-life balance. It allows you to recharge and return to work with a renewed sense of purpose.

Cultivates Long-Term Habits: Making movement a regular part of your lunchtime routine can help establish a habit of incorporating physical activity into your daily life. Consistency is key to reaping the long-term benefits of exercise.

Overall, moving at lunchtime is an important practice to prioritize your physical, mental, and emotional health. It can lead to increased productivity, improved mood, and a greater sense of well-being throughout the day.

Chapter 17

Dinner Time!

The Mediterranean eating pattern, which emphasizes consuming a larger meal in the evening and a smaller meal in the morning, is deeply rooted in cultural traditions and lifestyle habits. Several factors contribute to this dietary practice:

Climate and Lifestyle: In Mediterranean regions, the climate can be quite hot during the day, making heavy meals less appealing in the morning. Additionally, Mediterranean cultures often have a leisurely lunchtime, allowing for a more substantial midday meal.

Social and Family Dynamics: The Mediterranean culture places significant emphasis on family gatherings and communal meals. Dinner is considered a time for family and social interactions, providing an opportunity to enjoy a larger, more leisurely meal together.

Availability of Fresh Ingredients: Mediterranean countries have access to an abundance of fresh fruits, vegetables, and seafood. These nutrient-rich foods are often incorporated into the evening meal, contributing to its larger size and nutritional diversity.

In contrast, the eating patterns in the UK and USA are influenced by various cultural, societal, and historical factors, which have led to differences in meal sizes and timings:

On-the-Go Lifestyle: In modern Western societies, busy lifestyles and work schedules often lead to rushed breakfasts and limited time for midday meals. As a result, individuals may consume larger meals in the evening when they have more time to relax and enjoy their food.

Cultural Norms: In the UK and USA, there isn't a strong cultural tradition of eating a large midday meal. Instead, there is a cultural preference for larger dinners, especially for families who gather in the evenings.

Food Availability and Marketing: In the UK and USA, there is a wide availability of processed and convenience foods, which can lead to more frequent snacking and eating throughout the day. Food marketing and advertising also play a role in promoting larger portion sizes.

While it may be challenging for some people in the UK to adopt the "breakfast like a king, lunch like a prince, and dinner like a pauper" approach, there are several health benefits associated with this eating pattern:

Improved Digestion: Eating a smaller, lighter meal in the evening may promote better digestion and prevent discomfort while sleeping.

Better Blood Sugar Control: Consuming more calories earlier in the day and reducing evening calorie intake may help stabilize blood sugar levels and improve insulin sensitivity.

Weight Management: Studies suggest that eating larger meals earlier in the day and smaller meals in the evening may support weight management and reduce the risk of obesity.

Increased Energy: A balanced and nourishing breakfast can provide the energy needed to kickstart the day and support productivity.

Enhanced Sleep Quality: A lighter dinner can lead to improved sleep quality as the body focuses on resting and repairing rather than digesting heavy foods.

Here are seven dinner ideas with meat that are free of refined carbs, starch, and added sugars, and rich in fibre:

Grilled Chicken with Roasted Vegetables:

Grill lean organic chicken breast seasoned with herbs and spices and serve it with a colourful assortment of roasted vegetables like bell peppers, zucchini, and broccoli. Drizzle with olive oil for added flavour and healthy fats.

Baked Salmon with Asparagus and Quinoa:

Bake wild-caught salmon fillets colour of the salmon should be rich red) seasoned with lemon and dill, and serve it alongside steamed asparagus, peas and a side of quinoa. Quinoa provides protein and fibre, making it a nutritious grain alternative. Homemade oven baked sweet potato wedges are also delicious.

Stir-Fried Beef with Broccoli and Cauliflower Rice:

Make a flavourful stir-fry with lean beef strips, broccoli florets, and other colourful vegetables like red onion, red cabbage, bell peppers, bamboo shoots, sweetcorn, and snap peas. Serve over cauliflower rice for a low-carb and fibre-rich option.

Turkey Lettuce Wraps:

Cook organic ground turkey with garlic, ginger, and Asian-inspired seasonings, then serve the savoury mixture in crisp lettuce leaves. Add diced cucumbers, shredded carrots, and a drizzle of tahini sauce for extra flavour and texture.

Grilled Pork Chops with Grilled Vegetables:

Grill locally sourced juicy pork chops and pair them with a medley of grilled vegetables like eggplant, zucchini, and red onions. The charred veggies add a smoky flavour and plenty of fibre to the meal.

Baked Stuffed Bell Peppers:

Fill halved bell peppers with a mixture of lean ground beef, diced tomatoes, and sautéed onions and garlic. Top with a sprinkle of cheese and bake until tender and delicious.

Spaghetti Squash with Meatballs and Marinara:

Replace traditional pasta with spaghetti squash noodles for a low-carb alternative. Top with homemade meatballs and marinara sauce for a hearty and satisfying meal.

These dinner ideas provide a variety of meats, vegetables, and fibre-rich ingredients to keep your meals balanced, nutritious, and delicious without relying on refined carbs or starch. Enjoy exploring these flavourful and wholesome options as part of your healthy eating journey.

Catherine's Marinara Sauce:

Create a delicious and flavourful marinara sauce with these simple steps. Begin by dicing a medium white onion and sautéing it in butter. To avoid burning, add a splash of water and continue cooking until the onion turns translucent. Next, add a squished and finely chopped large garlic clove for added depth of flavour.

Once the onions and garlic are cooked to perfection, incorporate a can of chopped tomatoes, infusing the sauce with rich tomato goodness. Enhance the taste with a teaspoon of fragrant oregano and a dollop of tomato paste for extra richness. For a delightful touch, add a splash of red wine, Celtic salt, and pepper, allowing the flavours to harmonize.

Cover the sauce and let it simmer gently for about twenty minutes, ensuring the flavours meld together beautifully. Keep a watchful eye to maintain the ideal consistency and prevent overcooking.

Just before serving, elevate the sauce with torn fresh basil, imparting a delightful freshness. For the best flavour experience, it is recommended to let the sauce sit overnight, allowing the flavours to infuse and deepen.

When serving, generously sprinkle the sauce with grated parmesan cheese, enhancing its savoury richness and bringing it to a whole new level of deliciousness.

To elevate the sauce further, consider adding chopped crispy pancetta and juicy mushrooms for a hearty twist. Simply incorporate the sauce with these additional ingredients once they are fully cooked, resulting in a mouthwatering medley of flavours.

Enjoy Catherine's Marinara Sauce as a delightful accompaniment to chicken, or other dishes of your choice. With its savoury notes and versatility, this sauce is sure to become a staple in your culinary repertoire.

Here are seven low-carb, no-starch, no-sugar vegetarian dinner ideas that are rich in protein, healthy fats, oils, and fibre:

Zucchini Noodles with Pesto and Cherry Tomatoes:

Create zucchini noodles using a spiralizer and toss them with a homemade basil pesto sauce. Add halved cherry tomatoes and sprinkle with pine nuts or chopped almonds for added protein and crunch.

Cauliflower Fried Rice with Tofu:

Make a delicious cauliflower fried rice by pulsing cauliflower florets in a food processor until they resemble rice. Stir-fry the cauliflower "rice" with tofu, chopped vegetables, and scrambled eggs. Drizzle with sesame oil and low-sodium soy sauce for extra flavour.

Stuffed Bell Peppers with Lentils and Feta:

Cut the tops off bell peppers and remove the seeds. Fill the peppers with a mixture of cooked lentils, sautéed onions, garlic, and crumbled feta cheese. Bake until the peppers are tender, and the filling is hot.

Baked Eggplant Parmesan:

Layer thinly sliced eggplant with marinara sauce and mozzarella cheese in a baking dish. Top with a sprinkle of grated parmesan and bake until the cheese is bubbly and golden. Serve with a side salad for added fibre.

Portobello Mushroom Pizzas:

Roast portobello mushroom caps in the oven and then top them with marinara sauce, shredded mozzarella, and your favourite pizza toppings. Bake until the cheese is melted and bubbly.

Avocado and Chickpea Salad:

Create a refreshing salad with ripe avocado, chickpeas, cherry tomatoes, cucumbers, and red onion. Dress with a lemon-olive oil vinaigrette and garnish with fresh cilantro or parsley.

Grilled Halloumi with Asparagus and Lemon:

Grill halloumi cheese until it develops beautiful grill marks and serve it with roasted asparagus. Squeeze fresh lemon juice over the top for a zesty finish.

These dinner ideas offer a satisfying balance of protein, fats, oils, and fibre while keeping carbs to a minimum. They are not only delicious but also nutrient-dense, providing your body with the necessary nourishment for a healthy and well-rounded vegetarian diet. Enjoy exploring these flavourful options for your low-carb, no-starch, no-sugar vegetarian dinners.

Here are some additional side dishes that pair well with the mentioned low-carb, no-starch, no-sugar vegetarian dinner ideas:

Side Dish: Mixed Green Salad - Serve a fresh salad with a variety of mixed greens, cherry tomatoes, cucumbers, and a light vinaigrette dressing.

Side Dish: Steamed Broccoli - Steamed broccoli seasoned with a dash of garlic powder and a squeeze of lemon complements the savoury flavours of the cauliflower fried rice.

Side Dish: Quinoa Salad - Prepare a quinoa salad with diced bell peppers, cucumber, red onion, and a lemon-herb dressing for added protein and freshness.

Side Dish: Roasted Brussels Sprouts - Roast Brussels sprouts with olive oil, garlic, and a sprinkle of parmesan for a flavourful and nutritious side.

Side Dish: Caprese Salad - Enjoy a classic Caprese salad with slices of fresh mozzarella, ripe tomatoes, and basil leaves drizzled with balsamic glaze.

Side Dish: Roasted Sweet Potatoes - Roast sweet potato wedges with olive oil and your favourite herbs for a sweet and savoury accompaniment.

Side Dish: Greek Salad - Prepare a Greek salad with cucumbers, Kalamata olives, red onions, and feta cheese tossed in olive oil and red wine vinegar.

Chapter 18

Fishy on your Dishy!

Here are seven delicious and healthy oily fish dinners that are free from refined carbs, starch, bread, wheat, and sugar, while also being high in fibre: However, when choosing your fish be sure to eat wild caught fish and not farm bred fish, as wild fish are more nutrient dense, natural and an overall healthier product. Remember, whatever that fish has eaten, you are going to also eat!

Baked Salmon with Roasted Vegetables:

Season a salmon fillet with lemon, dill, and garlic, and then bake it in the oven. Serve the salmon with a side of roasted vegetables, such as broccoli, bell peppers, and zucchini, for added fibre and nutrients.

Grilled Mackerel with Quinoa and Steamed Greens:

Grill fresh mackerel with a squeeze of lemon and a sprinkle of sea salt. Serve the fish over a bed of fluffy quinoa and steamed greens, like spinach or kale, for a well-rounded and fibre-rich meal.

Pan-Seared Sardines with Avocado Salad:

Pan-sear sardine fillets with a touch of olive oil and garlic. Pair the sardines with a refreshing avocado salad, cherry tomatoes, cucumber, and red onion, dressed with a lemon-herb vinaigrette.

Tuna and Vegetable Stir-Fry:

Sauté canned tuna with a mix of colourful vegetables, such as bell peppers, snap peas, and carrots, in a light soy sauce and ginger dressing. Serve the stir-fry over cauliflower rice for a low-carb, high-fibre alternative.

Grilled Swordfish with Citrus Salsa:

Grill swordfish steaks and top them with a zesty citrus salsa made with oranges, grapefruits, cilantro, and jalapeños. Accompany the dish with a side of steamed asparagus or green beans.

Baked Haddock with Ratatouille:

Bake haddock fillets with a herb crust until golden and flaky. Pair the fish with a classic ratatouille made from eggplant, zucchini, tomatoes, and bell peppers, slowly simmered for a hearty and fibre-packed side.

Seared Trout with Lentil Salad:

Pan-sear trout fillets with a pinch of paprika and cumin for a smoky flavour. Serve the fish over a bed of warm lentil salad, mixed with diced cucumbers, cherry tomatoes, and fresh parsley.

These oily fish dinners are not only delicious but also nutrient-dense, providing you with essential omega-3 fatty acids, protein, and fibre.

TIP!

"Unmask the Truth: Nutrition Knowledge > Calorie Restrictions.

Recognizing how sugar affects the body enables smarter dietary decisions, surpassing the limitations of calorie counting."

Chapter 19

Plant Power!

Here are seven delicious and nutritious vegan dinners that are free from starch, bread, and refined carbs:

Grilled Portobello Mushrooms with Quinoa Salad:

Grill marinated portobello mushrooms and serve them over a quinoa salad with diced cucumbers, cherry tomatoes, red onion, and fresh herbs, dressed with lemon juice and olive oil.

Cauliflower Rice Stir-Fry:

Sauté cauliflower rice with a mix of colourful vegetables like bell peppers, broccoli, and snap peas, in a flavourful stir-fry sauce made with soy sauce, garlic, and ginger.

Vegan Lentil Shepherd's Pie:

Make a hearty shepherd's pie using cooked lentils, carrots, peas, and corn, topped with a creamy mashed cauliflower instead of traditional mashed potatoes.

"Sugar Savvy Squad: Unveiling Nutrition Wisdom"

Spinach and Cheese Omelette: A protein-packed meal perfect for any time of day.

Greek Yogurt Parfait: Layer yogurt, fruit, and a sprinkle of nuts for a nutritious dessert or snack.

Whole Wheat Pasta with Tomato Sauce: A simple, budget-friendly pasta dish made with whole ingredients.

Conclusion: Nourishing Wisdom for True Wellness

The "Sugar Savvy Squad" book isn't a fleeting trend but a beacon of wisdom that guides readers toward informed decisions. By advocating for mindful consumption, understanding the impacts of ultra-processed foods, and emphasizing the importance of cooking with whole ingredients, it charts a course to better health and well-being. In a world of noise, this book speaks the language of nourishment, both for the body and the mind.

Stuffed Bell Peppers with Mexican Quinoa:

Stuff bell peppers with a flavourful mixture of quinoa, black beans, diced tomatoes, corn, and avocado. Bake until the peppers are tender, and the filling is heated through.

Spaghetti Squash with Creamy Avocado Pesto:

Roast spaghetti squash and toss it with a creamy avocado pesto made with fresh basil, avocado, garlic, lemon juice, and a sprinkle of nutritional yeast for a cheesy flavour.

Vegan Chickpea Curry with Cauliflower Rice:

Prepare a rich and creamy chickpea curry using coconut milk and spices. Serve it over cauliflower rice and garnish with fresh cilantro and a squeeze of lime.

Grilled Eggplant Steaks with Chimichurri Sauce:

Grill thick eggplant slices and top them with a zesty chimichurri sauce made with parsley, cilantro, garlic, red pepper flakes, and olive oil.

These vegan dinners are not only delicious but also packed with nutrients, fibre, and plant-based protein. They offer a variety of flavours and textures while keeping starch and refined carbs off the plate. Enjoy these wholesome and satisfying meals as part of your balanced vegan diet.

"These are a selection of my homemade go-to dishes that have become a hit in our household. When I decided to go 'sugar-free,' I noticed some very positive changes in my physical and mental well-being. Since I no longer crave sweet foods, I have discovered a newfound appreciation for the flavours of vegetables, savouring them in a whole new way."

Berry Nutty Yogurt Bowl:

Combine 1 tablespoon of full-fat Greek yogurt with a generous amount of kefir.

Add a handful each of raspberries, blueberries, mixed nuts, and assorted seeds.

Top with pistachio nuts, broken pieces of 85% dark chocolate, chia seeds, and strawberries.

Avocado Toast with Scrambled Eggs and Brie:

Toast a slice of dark rye bread and drizzle with extra virgin olive oil.

Spread almond butter on the toast and top with scrambled eggs and chunks of Brie.

Add sliced avocado and sprinkle with Celtic salt and cayenne pepper.

Ricotta and Tomato Basil Toast:

Spread ricotta cheese on a slice of rye toast.

Layer with sliced tomatoes and fresh basil.

Drizzle with olive oil and season with salt and pepper.

Cherry Chia Seed Pudding:

In a bowl, mix fresh or frozen chopped cherries with a rounded tablespoon of full-fat Greek yogurt and a good glug of kefir.

Add 2 tablespoons of chia seeds and let it sit overnight to turn into a pudding.

Top with chopped almonds before serving.

Butter Bean Delight:

In a pan, sauté chopped shallots in butter, then add a teaspoon of red harissa paste.

Stir in a can of drained butter beans, a splash of milk, chopped parsley, salt, and pepper.

Serve with rye toast or fried eggs for a hearty meal.

Green Bean and Tomato Medley:

Fry a large onion, then add trimmed green beans, chili flakes, canned tomatoes, fresh parsley, salt, and pepper.

Cover and simmer for 15-20 minutes, and let it cool down. Optionally, use broad beans instead of green beans.

Mushroom Spinach Sauté:

In a pan, fry mushrooms and spinach in butter.

Add a teaspoon of French grain mustard and a dollop of yogurt, cream, or organic cream cheese.

Serve with quinoa or high-quality sourdough.

Decadent Hot Chocolate:

Melt three squares of 100 percent chocolate with milk in the microwave or pan.

Sweeten to taste, adding water and a pinch of salt. Adjust chocolate percentage to suit your preference.

Tuna-Stuffed Tomatoes:

Scoop out the inside of a tomato, chop and mix it with tuna, dollop of yogurt, salt, and pepper.

Stuff the mixture back into the tomatoes and serve.

Bournemouth Minestrone Soup:

Dice and fry white onion, garlic, carrots, celery, leek, and peas and one large celery stick in a large pan.

Add canned tomatoes, butter beans, cannellini beans, bay leaf oregano, pint of water, handful fresh chopped parsley, handful of torn fresh basil, salt, and pepper.

Simmer for an hour and serve the next day for the best flavour.

Classic Strawberries with Clotted Cream:

Simply enjoy fresh strawberries with clotted cream.

Chicken Soul Soup

- In a large pot, sauté the onion and garlic in butter over medium heat until softened.
- Add the carrots and celery to the pot and continue to cook for a few more minutes until the vegetables are slightly tender.
- Place the two organic chicken breasts on top of the vegetables in the pot.
- Pour the organic chicken stock over the chicken and vegetables.
- Add the bay leaf and a pinch of thyme to enhance the flavor.

- Cover the pot with a lid and let the soup simmer for about 45 minutes, allowing all the flavours to meld together.
- Check to ensure that the chicken breasts are fully cooked, then shred them into the soup using two forks.
- Season the soup with salt and pepper to your taste preference.

Milano Red Cabbage and Feta Cheese Salad:

Ingredients:

Grated red cabbage
Pink olives (Kalamata olives are often pinkish in colour)
Cubed feta cheese
Red wine vinegar
Olive oil
Salt and pepper
Instructions:

In a salad bowl, combine the grated red cabbage, pink olives, and cubes of feta cheese.
Drizzle the salad with red wine vinegar and olive oil.
Season with salt and pepper to taste.
Toss everything together until well mixed.
Serve and enjoy!

This colourful and tangy salad is perfect for a light and flavorful side dish. If you have any other favourite recipes or need further assistance, feel free to ask! Happy cooking!

Pretty in Pink Hummus Delight

Create a vibrant and nutritious Pink Barbie Girl Hummus with a touch of playfulness. In a blender, combine one drained can of kidney beans, along with two fresh or cooked beetroots for a stunning pink hue. Add a small clove of garlic, two dessert spoons of creamy tahini, a pinch of pink salt, a sprinkle of pink peppercorns, and a hint of lazy chili for a spicy kick (optional). Drizzle a teaspoon of extra virgin olive oil for added richness. Blend until smooth, then transfer the luscious hummus into a serving bowl. For a delightful crunch, top with pumpkin seeds and serve with an assortment of fresh vegetable sticks. A perfect blend of taste, color, and health in every bite!

Zesty Lemon Herb Dip

Savor the zing of lemon and the freshness of herbs with this delightful Zesty Lemon Herb Dip. In a bowl, combine Greek yogurt for creaminess, the zest and juice of one fresh lemon for a burst of flavor, and a pinch of sea salt for depth. Enhance the taste with freshly ground black pepper and add a generous amount of finely chopped fresh dill or mint leaves for an herbaceous twist. Mix everything together until the flavours meld into a harmonious dip. Enjoy this sugar-free dip with an assortment of crisp veggie sticks or as a light and flavorful dressing for salads. Satisfy your taste buds with this refreshing and health-conscious dip!

Grated Vegetable Salad:
Ingredients:

Half of a red cabbage, grated
2 large carrots, grated
2 large beetroots, grated
Himalayan pink salt
1 tablespoon of apple cider vinegar
A dash of olive oil
Instructions:

Grate the red cabbage, carrots, and beetroots, and transfer them to a mixing bowl.
Sprinkle Himalayan pink salt over the grated vegetables to taste.
Add a tablespoon of apple cider vinegar to the bowl.
Drizzle a dash of olive oil over the mixture.

Toss everything together until the vegetables are well-coated with the dressing.
Serve and enjoy the fresh and vibrant flavours!
This salad offers a delightful combination of colours and flavours, and the apple cider vinegar adds a pleasant tanginess to the mix. It's a great way to enjoy a healthy and satisfying dish.

"I also love Caprese Salad!-Catherine

Indulge in the classic and refreshing flavours of Caprese Salad with this easy-to-follow recipe:

Ingredients:

Fresh ripe tomatoes (any variety you prefer)
Fresh mozzarella cheese (buffalo mozzarella or regular)
Fresh basil leaves
Extra virgin olive oil
Sea salt and freshly ground black pepper to taste
Instructions:

Slice the Tomatoes: Wash the tomatoes and pat them dry. Cut the tomatoes into thick slices, about 1/4 inch in thickness.

Slice the Mozzarella: Drain any excess liquid from the mozzarella, and then cut it into slices similar in thickness to the tomatoes.

Assemble the Salad: On a serving platter or individual plates, arrange the tomato slices and mozzarella slices alternately, creating a visually appealing pattern.

Add Fresh Basil: Tuck fresh basil leaves between the tomato and mozzarella slices. You can use whole leaves or tear them into smaller pieces for even distribution.

Season and Dress: Drizzle extra virgin olive oil over the salad, ensuring it lightly coats the tomatoes and mozzarella. Season with a pinch of sea salt and freshly ground black pepper to taste.

Serve and Enjoy: Your Caprese Salad is now ready to be served. Enjoy it as a light and refreshing appetizer or side dish. It's a perfect complement to any meal, especially during hot summer days.

Tip: For an extra touch of elegance, you can also add a sprinkle of dried oregano or a drizzle of high-quality balsamic vinegar instead of the glaze.

This easy Caprese Salad recipe is sure to impress with its simplicity and delightful combination of fresh flavours. Enjoy the harmony of juicy tomatoes, creamy mozzarella, aromatic basil, and the richness of olive oil. Buon appetito!

"Annie's Pippande"

Treat yourself to the delightful flavours of Annie's Pippande, a simple and versatile homemade dish that will leave you craving more. This vegan-friendly recipe is quick and easy, making it a perfect addition to any meal.

Ingredients:

1 large onion, thinly sliced
2 tablespoons butter (or vegan butter for a plant-based option)
1 red bell pepper, thinly sliced
1 yellow bell pepper, thinly sliced
1 green bell pepper, thinly sliced
1 can of diced tomatoes
A glug of red wine (optional)

Salt and pepper to taste
Instructions:

Sauté the Onions: In a large skillet, melt the butter over medium heat. Add the thinly sliced onion and cook until soft and translucent.

Add the Bell Peppers: Stir in the red, yellow, and green bell peppers, and continue cooking until they become tender.

Incorporate Tomatoes and Red Wine: Pour the diced tomatoes into the skillet, along with a glug of red wine if desired. Season with salt and pepper to taste.

Simmer and Serve: Let the mixture simmer for about 20 minutes, allowing the flavours to meld together. The dish is ready when the peppers are tender, and the sauce has thickened slightly.

Enjoy the Magic: Annie's Pippande is now ready to be savored! Serve it hot and enjoy the wonderful combination of flavours. For an even richer taste, let it cool and reheat the next day—this dish tastes even better with time!

Annie's Pippande is a versatile delight that pairs well with various accompaniments. Enjoy it as a side dish or toss it over pasta, rice, or quinoa for a hearty and wholesome meal. This simple yet flavorful recipe is a must-try for any food lover!

TIP!
"Beyond Weight: Sugar's Influence on Body and Mind.

Sugar's effects extend to disrupting hormones, triggering inflammation, and hindering mental clarity, beyond weight gain."

Sun-Dried Tomato Hummus with peanut butter:

Ingredients:

1 jar of sun-dried tomatoes in olive oil
1 can of chickpeas, drained
1 tablespoon of palm oil-free peanut butter
1 small clove of garlic
Splash of water
Salt and pepper to taste
Instructions:

In a food processor or blender, add the jar of sun-dried tomatoes (including the olive oil), drained chickpeas, palm oil-free peanut butter, and the clove of garlic.
Season with salt and pepper to your preferred taste.
Blend all the ingredients until smooth and creamy, adjusting the seasoning if needed.

If the hummus is too thick, you can add a splash of water or more olive oil to achieve your desired consistency.
Transfer the sun-dried tomato hummus to a serving bowl. You can garnish it with a drizzle of olive oil, some chopped sun-dried tomatoes, or a sprinkle of paprika for an extra touch of flavor.
Serve the hummus vegetable sticks.
This sun-dried tomato hummus is a delightful twist on the classic hummus, and the addition of sun-dried tomatoes gives it a rich and tangy flavor. Enjoy this delicious and nutritious dip as a snack or appetizer.

Important note from Catherine

"Plant foods need to be combined strategically to create complete amino acid chains because most individual plant sources are deficient in one or more essential amino acids required by the human body. A complete amino acid chain consists of all nine essential amino acids that the body cannot produce on its own and must be obtained through diet. By combining specific plant foods that complement each other's amino acid profiles, individuals following a vegan diet can ensure they receive all the essential amino acids necessary for optimal health and protein synthesis.

Here are seven examples of how vegans can combine certain plant foods to obtain all the essential amino acids:

Beans and Rice: Legumes like beans, lentils, and chickpeas are rich in lysine but lack sufficient methionine. On the other hand, rice is low in lysine but has a good amount of methionine. Combining beans and rice in a meal provides a complete amino acid profile.

Hummus and Whole Wheat Pita: Chickpeas, used to make hummus, are high in lysine and low in methionine. Pairing hummus with whole wheat pita, which is higher in methionine, creates a balanced amino acid intake.

Quinoa and Mixed Vegetables: Quinoa is unique among grains as it contains all the essential amino acids. Pairing it with a variety of mixed vegetables enhances the overall amino acid profile and nutrient content.

Tofu or Tempeh and Grains: Soy-based products like tofu or tempeh are good sources of lysine. When combined with whole grains like quinoa, brown rice, or whole wheat, which are richer in methionine, a complete amino acid chain is achieved.

Lentils and Whole Wheat Bread: Lentils are a good source of lysine but lack sufficient methionine. Pairing them with whole wheat bread, which has a better methionine content, creates a balanced amino acid intake.

Nuts and Seeds with Whole Grain Cereal: Nuts and seeds, such as almonds, pumpkin seeds, and chia seeds, are rich in methionine. Adding them to a bowl of whole grain cereal or oatmeal, which contains lysine, ensures a complete amino acid profile.

Nut Butter on Whole Grain Bread: Nut butters, such as peanut or almond butter, are high in methionine. Spreading them on whole grain bread, which has lysine, offers a complete set of essential amino acids.

It's important to note that while traditionally it was believed that nine essential amino acids needed to be combined, recent research suggests that our understanding of amino acid requirements is more nuanced. The body has a "pool" of amino acids that it draws from over time, so it's not necessary to combine specific foods in every meal. As long as a variety of plant-based protein sources are included throughout the day, the body can effectively utilize the available amino acids to support its needs.

In conclusion, combining plant foods strategically can help vegans obtain all the essential amino acids necessary for proper health and protein synthesis. While there are examples of combining foods to create complete amino acid profiles, the modern understanding of amino acid requirements indicates that a varied diet over the course of the day can sufficiently provide the necessary amino acids for the body's needs."

Chapter 20

Smooth Operator

It's completely understandable that you may not be a fan of smoothies due to certain concerns and preferences. Let me explain the reasons behind your viewpoint:

"A smoothie can serve as a convenient and appealing option for individuals who struggle to consume vegetables they may not particularly enjoy, offering a palatable way to obtain essential nutrients and promote their overall health."

Slow Food to Fast Food: Traditional slow foods involve taking the time to prepare and savor meals, emphasizing the natural textures and flavours of whole ingredients. In contrast, smoothies are often quick and convenient, blending various ingredients into a homogeneous texture. This fast transformation can diminish the experience of appreciating the individual components of the meal.

Molecular Structure of Plants: Some argue that blending fruits and vegetables into smoothies can potentially break down the cell walls, altering the molecular structure of the plants. This, in turn, might impact the absorption of nutrients and certain health benefits compared to eating the whole fruits and veggies in their natural state.

Struggling to Eat Greens: Despite the desire to eat more greens for their nutritional benefits, some individuals find it challenging to consume them in their regular diet. Smoothies can be a practical solution to incorporate a variety of nutrient-rich greens into the diet more easily.

Protein-Focused Smoothie: Opting for a protein-inspired smoothie with greens can be a healthier alternative to fruit-heavy smoothies that may contain higher concentrations of natural sugars. This protein-focused approach can help stabilize blood glucose levels and provide a more balanced and filling meal option.

In summary, while smoothies might not align with certain slow food principles and concerns about the molecular structure of plants, they can still serve as a practical means to increase nutrient intake, particularly when it comes to incorporating greens into one's diet. Choosing a protein-rich smoothie with greens can help mitigate potential spikes in blood glucose levels often associated with fruit-heavy smoothies.

As with any dietary choice, it's essential to consider individual preferences, health goals, and concerns while exploring different ways to obtain essential nutrients. A balanced approach to nutrition that works well for you is key, and there are numerous ways to incorporate greens and other nutrient-dense foods into your daily meals based on your personal tastes and values.

Certainly! Here's an original response explaining why shop-bought smoothies can be unhealthy:

Shop-bought smoothies can be deemed unhealthy for several reasons:

High Sugar Content: Many commercially available smoothies are loaded with added sugars or sweetened fruit juices to enhance taste. These extra sugars can lead to spikes in blood sugar levels and contribute to weight gain and other health concerns.

Reduced Fiber Content: During the blending process, some shop-bought smoothies lose the natural fiber present in whole fruits and vegetables. Fiber is essential for proper digestion and helps regulate blood sugar levels.

Calorie Overload: Certain store-bought smoothies can be calorie-dense due to the larger portion sizes and the addition of ingredients like sugary syrups, frozen yogurt, or high-fat nut butters.

Poor Nutrient Balance: While smoothies may contain fruits and vegetables, they might not offer a well-rounded nutrient profile. Some commercial versions lack essential nutrients and may contain high amounts of sugar and unhealthy fats.

Presence of Preservatives and Additives: To extend shelf life and enhance flavor, shop-bought smoothies may include preservatives, artificial flavours, and other additives that can be detrimental to health.

Lack of Portion Control: It's easy to consume a significant number of calories and sugar in one sitting when drinking store-bought smoothies, potentially leading to overeating and weight gain.

Misleading Marketing: Smoothies labeled as "healthy" may still contain hidden sugars and unhealthy ingredients, necessitating careful scrutiny of labels.

To ensure a healthier smoothie option, consider making them at home using whole, fresh ingredients. By doing so, you can control the sugar content, incorporate a diverse range of nutrient-rich foods, and benefit from the fiber and natural nutrients found in whole fruits and vegetables. Homemade smoothies offer a better balance of nutrients without the concealed additives and excessive sugars commonly found in store-bought versions.

Here's my "Green Means Go" Smoothie

Ingredients:

240ml kefir
120ml Greek yogurt (for added creaminess and protein)
240ml fresh spinach leaves
1/2 cucumber, peeled and chopped
1/2 avocado, peeled and pitted
1/2 banana
1 tablespoon chia seeds or flax seeds (for extra protein and nutrients)
Ice cubes (optional, for a chilled smoothie)
Instructions:

In a blender, combine kefir, Greek yogurt, fresh spinach, chopped cucumber, avocado, and ripe banana.
Add chia seeds or hemp seeds for an additional protein boost.
If you prefer a sweeter taste, add a teaspoon of honey or maple syrup.
Blend all the ingredients until smooth and creamy. You can add a few ice cubes if you like a chilled smoothie.
Pour the high-protein kefir smoothie into a glass and enjoy its nutritious goodness.
This high-protein kefir smoothie is not only delicious but also packed with essential nutrients from green vegetables. It's an excellent choice for a nutritious and energizing breakfast or a post-workout refuel. Feel free to customize the ingredients or adjust the sweetness according to your taste preferences. Enjoy your healthy and green-filled smoothie!

Graziella's Chocolate Avocado Mousse with Sugar-Free Coconut Cream

Experience the delight of a guilt-free treat with this velvety chocolate avocado mousse that boasts both creaminess and a sugar-free profile. The infusion of coconut cream introduces a tropical nuance that elevates the flavor. This recipe yields 2 servings.

Ingredients:

2 ripe avocados, peeled and pitted
25 grams of unsweetened cocoa powder

Teaspoon maple syrup
60 milliliters of coconut cream
1 teaspoon of vanilla extract
Pinch of salt
Optional toppings: shaved dark chocolate, fresh berries, chopped nuts

Instructions:

In a food processor or blender, combine the peeled and pitted ripe avocados, unsweetened cocoa powder, sugar-free sweetener, coconut cream, vanilla extract, and a pinch of salt.

Blend the mixture until it transforms into a smooth and luxurious consistency. Pause occasionally to scrape down the sides, ensuring a thorough and cohesive blend.

Taste the mixture and fine-tune the sweetness according to your personal preference. If required, incorporate additional amounts of the chosen sugar-free sweetener and blend once more.

With the mousse now achieving a silky texture, gently spoon it into serving glasses or bowls.

Allow the mousse to chill and the flavors to meld by refrigerating it for a minimum of 30 minutes.

When ready to serve, consider garnishing the mousse with shaved dark chocolate, a handful of fresh berries, chopped nuts, or any other toppings that resonate with your taste.

Relish in the exquisite flavor and texture of your homemade chocolate avocado mousse, complemented by the nuances of sugar-free coconut cream.

Remember, if the consistency of the mousse feels excessively thick, you can introduce a small amount of unsweetened almond milk or coconut milk while blending to reach your desired texture. It's worth noting that the flavors within the mousse tend to intensify during the chilling process, making it potentially even more delectable after some time in the refrigerator.

TIP!
"Say No to Fads: Educate Yourself for Long-Term Health.

Nutritional education is a sustainable approach, countering trendy diets and addressing sugar intake's impact."

Chapter 21

More Dish Ideas

Organic Minced Beef and Quinoa Delight:

Ingredients:

200g quinoa
15g butter
1 large onion, diced
2 cloves of garlic, minced
1 red bell pepper, chopped
200g mushrooms, chopped (or 1 can of peas, if preferred)

500g minced beef or Quorn if vegan
400g can of chopped tomatoes
A glug of red wine (approximately 50ml)
Salt and pepper to taste
1 teaspoon mixed herbs
1 tablespoon tomato puree
1 bay leaf
Grated Parmesan/vegan cheese, for topping
Optional: Lazy chili for added flavor

Instructions:

Rinse the quinoa under cold water and cook it in a pot with 400ml of water. Bring to a boil, then reduce the heat to a high simmer, and cook for 15 minutes or until the quinoa is tender and the water is absorbed.
While the quinoa is cooking, melt the butter in a large pan. Add the diced onion and minced garlic, and sauté until softened.
Add the chopped red bell pepper and mushrooms (or peas if using) to the pan. Cook until they are tender.
Stir in the minced beef and cook until browned and fully cooked.
Pour in the can of chopped tomatoes and a glug of red wine. Season with salt, pepper, and mixed herbs.
Add the cooked quinoa, tomato puree, and bay leaf to the pan. Mix everything together.
Let the mixture simmer for 15 minutes, stirring occasionally. Keep an eye on the consistency and adjust the seasoning if needed.
Once cooked, allow the dish to cool slightly before serving. Its best the next day!
Grate Parmesan cheese over the top for an extra burst of flavor.

For added kick, you can optionally serve it with a sprinkle of lazy chili and a pinch of cinnamon.

This delightful, minced beef and quinoa dish is a comforting and filling meal that can be enjoyed both fresh and leftovers. It's a versatile recipe that you can customize to your taste preferences by adding a hint of chili and cinnamon for a delightful twist. Enjoy this nutritious and flavorful dish on a cold morning or any time you crave a satisfying meal.

Date Night Dining

Date night options for starters, mains, and desserts:

Starters:

- Smoked Salmon Cucumber Bites: Delicately rolled smoked salmon slices filled with a mixture of cream cheese, fresh dill, and lemon zest, served on thinly sliced cucumber rounds.

- Avocado Caprese Salad: Slices of ripe avocado layered with fresh mozzarella, ripe tomatoes, and basil leaves, drizzled with balsamic glaze and olive oil.
- Zucchini Carpaccio: Thinly sliced zucchini marinated in olive oil, lemon juice, and a touch of garlic, garnished with shaved Parmesan cheese and fresh arugula.

Mains:

- Grilled Herb-Marinated Chicken: Succulent chicken breasts marinated in a mixture of olive oil, garlic, rosemary, and thyme, then grilled to perfection and served with a side of sautéed spinach.
- Cauliflower Steak with Mushroom Ragout: Thick slices of roasted cauliflower steak topped with a rich mushroom and herb ragout, accompanied by a side of steamed asparagus.
- Pan-Seared Salmon with Avocado Salsa: Pan-seared salmon fillets topped with a refreshing salsa made from diced avocado, cherry tomatoes, red onion, cilantro, and lime juice, served with a side of roasted Brussels sprouts.

Desserts:

- Berry Parfait: Layers of mixed berries (such as strawberries, blueberries, and raspberries) and unsweetened Greek yogurt, topped with a sprinkle of crushed nuts or seeds for added texture.

- Chocolate Avocado Mousse: A velvety mousse made from ripe avocados, unsweetened cocoa powder, a touch of almond milk, and a hint of vanilla, sweetened with a natural sugar substitute like maple syrup.
- Coconut Chia Pudding: Creamy chia pudding made by soaking chia seeds in coconut milk and vanilla extract overnight, topped with toasted coconut flakes and a few fresh berries.
- These options provide a balance of flavors and textures while keeping sugar and carbs in check, ensuring a romantic and enjoyable evening without compromising on health-conscious choices.

A sugar-free children's birthday party buffet. Warning does contain nuts, adjust accordingly!

Savory Items:

- Mini Veggie Frittatas: Bite-sized frittatas packed with colorful veggies and cheese.
- Zucchini Pizza Bites: Zucchini slices topped with tomato sauce, veggies, and cheese, baked until bubbly.
- Mini Chicken Lettuce Wraps: Lettuce leaves filled with seasoned chicken and crunchy veggies.

- Quinoa Stuffed Bell Peppers: Bell peppers stuffed with quinoa, black beans, and spices.
- Rainbow Veggie Skewers: Skewers loaded with cherry tomatoes, bell peppers, cucumber, and a sprinkle of feta.
- Crispy Baked Cauliflower: Cauliflower florets coated in a flavorful seasoning and baked until crispy.
- Mini Caprese Skewers: Skewers with mini mozzarella balls, cherry tomatoes, and fresh basil.
- Veggie Spring Rolls: Rice paper rolls filled with julienned veggies and served with a dipping sauce.
- Hummus Stuffed Cucumbers: Cucumber slices hollowed out and filled with hummus and chopped veggies.
- Sweet Potato Bites: Roasted sweet potato rounds topped with avocado and salsa.

Healthy Dips:

- Creamy Spinach Dip: A creamy dip made with spinach, Greek yogurt, and herbs.
- Fresh Mango Salsa: A fruity salsa with diced mango, red onion, cilantro, and lime.
- Carrot and White Bean Dip: Dip made with cooked white beans, carrots, lemon juice, and garlic.
- Avocado and Lime Dip: Creamy avocado dip with a squeeze of lime and a pinch of salt.
- Cauliflower Hummus: Hummus made with cauliflower as the base, served with veggie sticks.

- Cucumber and Dill Yogurt Dip: Greek yogurt dip infused with fresh cucumber and dill.
- Black Bean Guacamole: Guacamole with added black beans for extra protein and fiber.
- Sundried Tomato Tapenade: Tapenade made with sundried tomatoes, olives, and herbs.
- Roasted Red Pepper and Walnut Dip: Dip with roasted red peppers, walnuts, and a touch of cumin.
- Cilantro Lime Yogurt Dip: Tangy yogurt dip with cilantro, lime juice, and a dash of cayenne.

Sugar-Free Desserts:

- Berry Parfait Cups: Layered Greek yogurt and mixed berry parfaits in mini cups.
- Chia Seed Pudding: Chia seed pudding made with almond milk and topped with fresh fruit.
- Coconut Bliss Balls: Bliss balls made with dates, coconut, and a hint of cocoa powder.
- Apple Nachos: Apple slices drizzled with almond butter and topped with shredded coconut.
- Frozen Fruit Skewers: Skewers with frozen grapes, melon, and berries.

- Chocolate-Dipped Strawberries: Strawberries dipped in melted dark chocolate and chilled.
- Mini Banana Muffins: Mini muffins made with ripe bananas and whole-grain flour.
- Yogurt Berry Bark: Greek yogurt spread on a baking sheet and topped with berries before freezing.
- Fruit Kabobs with Yogurt Dip: Fruit kabobs served with a side of Greek yogurt. (Add a smidge of honey, as the yogurt could taste "way too bitter" for kids)
- Mini Watermelon Slices: Watermelon wedges cut into mini triangles for easy snacking.
- Sugar-Free Drinks:

- Fruit-Infused Water: Chilled water infused with slices of citrus fruits, berries, and herbs.
- Cucumber Mint Sparkler: Sparkling water mixed with fresh cucumber slices and mint leaves.
- Berry Blast Smoothie: A smoothie made with mixed berries, milk, and ice.
- Iced Herbal Tea Punch: Herbal tea chilled with ice and a splash of freshly squeezed juice.
- Coconut Pineapple Cooler: Coconut water blended with fresh pineapple chunks and ice.
- Sparkling Fruit Spritzer: Sparkling water mixed with a splash of unsweetened fruit juice.
- Green Goodness Smoothie: A green smoothie with spinach, avocado, and coconut water.
- Hibiscus Iced Tea: Iced hibiscus tea with a squeeze of lemon and a drop of liquid stevia.

Party Favors:

- Colorful Play Dough: Homemade play dough in small containers with natural food coloring.
- Seeds: Packets of flower seeds to take home
- DIY Nature Craft Kits: Kits with materials like pinecones, twine, and feathers for crafting.
- T-shirt Craft: Create designs on T-shirts to take home.
- Mini Coloring Books: Mini coloring books with non-toxic crayons or colored pencils.
- Homemade Fruit Snacks: Make your own gummy fruit snacks using natural fruit juices.
- Mini Water Bottles: Small, reusable water bottles with fun designs and colors.
- Mindfulness Activity Cards: Cards with simple mindfulness exercises for kids to practice.
- Healthy Snack Packs: Mini packs with mixed nuts, seeds, and dried fruits for snacking.
- Decorate-Your-Own Tote Bags: Plain canvas tote bags and fabric markers for creative fun.

Here are three dinner party menus tailored to different dietary preferences (carnivore, vegetarian, vegan), with an emphasis on being sugar-free:

Carnivore Dinner Party:

Starter:

Prosciutto-Wrapped Asparagus: Crisp asparagus spears wrapped in prosciutto, lightly grilled and drizzled with olive oil and balsamic vinegar reduction.
Main Course:

2. Grilled Lemon Herb Chicken: Juicy chicken breasts marinated in a blend of lemon juice, herbs, and olive oil. Grilled to perfection and served with roasted garlic Brussels sprouts.

Side Dish:
3. Creamed Spinach: Sautéed spinach in a creamy sauce made with coconut milk, dairy-free butter, and a touch of nutritional yeast.

Dessert:
4. Mixed Berry Parfait: Layers of fresh mixed berries (strawberries, raspberries, blueberries) topped with a dollop of coconut whipped cream and chopped mint.

Vegetarian Dinner Party:

Starter:

Roasted Red Pepper Hummus with Veggie Sticks: Creamy roasted red pepper hummus served with an assortment of colorful vegetable sticks for dipping.
Main Course:
2. Eggplant Parmesan: Slices of eggplant coated with a gluten-free breadcrumb mixture, baked until crispy, and layered with marinara sauce and dairy-free mozzarella.

Side Dish:
3. Zucchini Noodles with Pesto: Fresh zucchini noodles tossed in homemade basil pesto made with pine nuts, olive oil, and nutritional yeast.

Dessert:
4. Coconut Chia Pudding with Berries: Chia pudding made with coconut milk and served with a medley of fresh berries and a sprinkle of unsweetened shredded coconut.

Vegan Dinner Party:

Starter:

Crispy Cauliflower Bites: Cauliflower florets coated in a gluten-free chickpea flour batter, seasoned with spices, and baked until crispy. Served with dairy-free yogurt dipping sauce.

Main Course:
2. Chickpea and Vegetable Stir-Fry: A colorful stir-fry made with chickpeas, bell peppers, snap peas, and broccoli, tossed in a sesame-ginger sauce. Served over quinoa.

Side Dish:
3. Cauliflower Rice Pilaf: Cauliflower rice cooked with sautéed onions, garlic, and a mix of chopped nuts and fresh herbs.

Dessert:

4. Avocado Chocolate Mousse: Creamy chocolate mousse made with ripe avocados, unsweetened cocoa powder, vanilla extract, and a touch of almond milk.

These menus should provide a variety of sugar-free options for your dinner party, tailored to different dietary preferences. Enjoy your gatherings!

Chapter 22

Desserts

Transitioning to a healthier diet often involves reducing our dependency on overly sweet or processed desserts. However, it doesn't mean we have to completely give up on the joy of enjoying delectable treats. By making homemade, natural, and less processed puddings and desserts, we can treat ourselves occasionally without compromising our health goals. Here are some points to explain this further:

Less Refined Sugars: Homemade desserts allow us to control the sweetness level by using natural sweeteners like honey, maple syrup, or fruit-based sweeteners, which are less refined and contain more nutrients compared to processed sugars.

Whole Ingredients: Preparing homemade puddings and desserts gives us the opportunity to use whole, unprocessed ingredients like fresh fruits, nuts, seeds, and natural fats, which provide essential nutrients and contribute to a balanced diet.

Reduced Additives: Store-bought ultra-processed desserts often contain additives, preservatives, and artificial flavours that are not ideal for our health. By making treats at home, we can avoid these additives and enjoy a purer, more nourishing dessert experience.

Mindful Indulgence: Occasional homemade treats allow us to practice mindful indulgence. By savoring and appreciating these delightful desserts, we can truly enjoy the experience and avoid mindless overconsumption.

Creative Freedom: Preparing homemade puddings and desserts gives us the freedom to experiment with flavours, textures, and ingredients, making the experience more exciting and personalized.

Balanced Lifestyle: Moderation is key. Enjoying homemade, natural treats occasionally can be part of a balanced lifestyle that prioritizes nourishment while still allowing for enjoyment and pleasure in our eating habits.

Positive Relationship with Food: By choosing homemade and healthier desserts, we develop a positive relationship with food, focusing on nourishing our bodies while indulging in the joy of delicious flavours.

Ultimately, the goal is to move away from dependence on overly sweet and processed desserts and embrace a more wholesome approach to treating ourselves. By opting for homemade delights filled with nature's goodness, we can satisfy our taste buds, nourish our bodies, and enjoy a more sustainable and balanced relationship with food.

Chia Seed Pudding:

Ingredients:
60g chia seeds
240ml unsweetened almond milk or coconut milk
1 teaspoon vanilla extract
A pinch of cinnamon
Fresh berries for topping
Coconut Avocado Mousse:

Ingredients:
1 ripe avocado
60ml coconut cream
15g unsweetened cocoa powder
1/2 teaspoon vanilla extract

A pinch of salt

Greek Yogurt with Nuts and Berries:

Ingredients:
240ml plain Greek yogurt (unsweetened)
Handful of mixed nuts (e.g., almonds, walnuts, pistachios)
Handful of fresh berries (e.g., strawberries, blueberries, raspberries)

Baked Apples with Sri Lanka Cinnamon:

Ingredients:
4 medium-sized apples
1 teaspoon ground cinnamon
1/4 teaspoon ground nutmeg
A drizzle of almond butter or coconut oil

Peanut Butter and Banana Pudding:

Ingredients:
2 ripe bananas
2 tablespoons natural peanut butter (sugar-free)

A sprinkle of unsweetened cocoa powder or chopped nuts (optional)

Cocoa and Coconut Milk Pudding:

Ingredients:
240ml unsweetened coconut milk
2 tablespoons unsweetened cocoa powder
Teeny bit of honey
A pinch of salt
Shredded coconut for garnish

Berries and Cream:

Ingredients:
Mixed fresh berries (e.g., strawberries, raspberries, blackberries)
240ml whipped coconut cream (whip the solid part of chilled canned coconut milk) or use clotted cream!

These delicious no-sugar, no-starch, and no-refined carb pudding ideas are perfect for satisfying your sweet cravings while maintaining a balanced and healthy diet. Enjoy experimenting with these recipes and adjusting them to suit your taste preferences!

Hot Cakes!

Blueberry Almond Pudding:

Ingredients:

100g almond flour
2 large eggs
2 tablespoons almond butter
Smidge of honey
A handful of fresh blueberries
Method:

Preheat the oven to 180°C (350°F) and grease a baking dish.

In a bowl, mix almond flour, eggs, almond butter, and a smidge of honey

Gently fold in the fresh blueberries.

Pour the mixture into the prepared baking dish and bake for about 20-25 minutes or until set and slightly golden.

Carrot Almond Pudding:

Ingredients:

100g almond flour
2 large eggs
2 tablespoons almond butter
1 medium carrot, grated
1 teaspoon ground Sri Lanka cinnamon
Method:

Preheat the oven to 180°C (350°F) and grease a baking dish.

In a bowl, mix almond flour, eggs, almond butter, grated carrot, and ground cinnamon until well combined.
Pour the mixture into the prepared baking dish and bake for about 25-30 minutes or until cooked through.

Zucchini Nut Butter Pudding:

Ingredients:

100g almond flour
2 large eggs
2 tablespoons nut butter
1 medium zucchini, grated
A pinch of salt
Method:

Preheat the oven to 180°C (350°F) and grease a baking dish.

In a bowl, mix almond flour, eggs, nut butter, grated zucchini, and a pinch of salt until well combined.
Pour the mixture into the prepared baking dish and bake for about 25-30 minutes or until firm and muffin-like.

Raspberry Almond Muffin Pudding:

Ingredients:

100g almond flour
2 large eggs
2 tablespoons almond butter
A handful of raspberries
Method:

Preheat the oven to 180°C (350°F) and line muffin cups with paper liners.
In a blender, blend almond flour, eggs, almond butter, and raspberries until smooth.
Pour the mixture into the prepared muffin cups and bake for about 20-25 minutes or until risen and lightly golden.

100g almond flour
2 large eggs
2 tablespoons nut butter (e.g., almond or peanut butter)
A handful of fresh spinach leaves
1/2 teaspoon vanilla extract
Method:

Preheat the oven to 180°C (350°F) and grease a baking dish.
In a blender, blend almond flour, eggs, nut butter, fresh spinach leaves, and vanilla extract until smooth.

Pour the mixture into the prepared baking dish and bake for about 20-25 minutes or until cooked through.

Blackberry Almond Bread Pudding:

Ingredients:

100g almond flour
2 large eggs
2 tablespoons almond butter
A handful of blackberries
1/2 teaspoon ground cinnamon
Method:

Preheat the oven to 180°C (350°F) and grease a baking dish.
In a bowl, mix almond flour, eggs, almond butter, blackberries, and ground cinnamon until well combined.

Pour the mixture into the prepared baking dish and bake for about 25-30 minutes or until firm and bread pudding-like.

Sweet Potato Almond Muffin Pudding:

Ingredients:

100g almond flour
2 large eggs
2 tablespoons nut butter (e.g., almond or peanut butter)
1 medium sweet potato, cooked and mashed
A pinch of ground nutmeg
Method:

Preheat the oven to 180°C (350°F) and line muffin cups with paper liners.
In a bowl, mix almond flour, eggs, nut butter, mashed sweet potato, and ground nutmeg until well combined.

Pour the mixture into the prepared muffin cups and bake for about 20-25 minutes or until risen and cooked through.
8. Strawberry Almond Pudding:

Ingredients:

100g almond flour
2 large eggs
2 tablespoons almond butter
A handful of strawberries
1/2 teaspoon vanilla extract
Method:

Preheat the oven to 180°C (350°F) and grease a baking dish.
In a blender, blend almond flour, eggs, almond butter, strawberries, and vanilla extract until smooth.
Pour the mixture into the prepared baking dish and bake for about 20 minutes.
Mint Chocolate Chip Cottage Cheese Ice Cream:

Ingredients:

500g cottage cheese
1/4 cup fresh mint leaves
1 teaspoon peppermint extract
2 tablespoons dark chocolate chips
Method:

In a blender or food processor, blend cottage cheese, mint leaves, peppermint extract, and chocolate chips until smooth.
Pour the mixture into an ice cream maker and churn according to the manufacturer's instructions.

Transfer the churned ice cream to a container and freeze until firm.

These cottage cheese ice cream recipes are easy to prepare, require minimal sweeteners, and are packed with flavor. Enjoy these guilt-free frozen treats that are both nutritious and delicious!

Vegan Ice cream

Creamy Vegan Chocolate Protein Ice Cream:

Ingredients:
2 cups frozen banana slices (about 340g)
25g plant-based protein powder (chocolate-flavored)
25g unsweetened cocoa powder
120ml unsweetened almond milk
15g almond butter
5ml vanilla extract
A pinch of salt

Creamy Vegan Vanilla Almond Protein Ice Cream:

Ingredients:
2 cups frozen banana slices (about 340g)
25g plant-based protein powder (vanilla-flavored)
120ml unsweetened almond milk (or any plant-based milk)
15g almond butter
5ml vanilla extract
A pinch of salt

Vegan Raspberry Coconut Protein Ice Cream:

Ingredients:
2 cups frozen raspberries (about 280g)
25g plant-based protein powder (vanilla or unflavored)
120ml coconut cream

Method:

For all recipes, follow the same method:

In a blender or food processor, blend the frozen fruit with the plant-based protein powder and other ingredients until smooth and creamy.
Transfer the mixture to an ice cream maker and churn according to the manufacturer's instructions.
Once churned, transfer the ice cream to a container and freeze until firm.

TIP!
"Sugar: The Hidden Culprit Behind Physical and Mental Struggles.

Excessive sugar consumption can lead to mood swings, fatigue, and cognitive challenges, affecting both body and mind".

Chapter 23

Top Tips to Wellness

Herbs

Add Fresh Herbs to Salads: Chop and sprinkle fresh herbs like basil, parsley, cilantro, mint, or dill over your salads. They not only add a burst of flavor but also enhance the nutritional value of your greens.

Make Herb Pesto: Create a delicious and versatile herb pesto using basil, parsley, or cilantro. Blend the herbs with garlic, nuts or seeds, olive oil, and a bit of lemon juice. Use the pesto as a pasta sauce, salad dressing, or sandwich spread.

Enhance Soups and Stews: Stir in freshly chopped herbs like thyme, rosemary, or oregano into your soups and stews to infuse them with rich flavours.

Herb-Infused Oils: Make your own herb-infused oils by steeping fresh herbs in olive oil. Drizzle the flavored oil over dishes for an extra layer of taste.

Herb Butter: Mix finely chopped herbs with softened butter or plant-based alternatives. Use this herb butter to top cooked vegetables, grilled meat, or bread.

Marinades: Create herb-based marinades with a combination of fresh herbs, garlic, citrus juice, and olive oil. Marinate meats, tofu, or vegetables to tenderize and flavor them.

Herb Garnishes: Use fresh herbs as a beautiful and tasty garnish for your dishes. Sprinkle chopped chives on scrambled eggs, add a basil leaf to caprese salad, or place cilantro on top of your tacos.

Herb-Infused Water or Tea: Infuse water or tea with fresh herbs like mint, basil, or lemon verbena for a refreshing and flavorful drink.

Herb Blends: Create your own herb blends by mixing various herbs together. Store the blends in an airtight container and use them as seasoning for various dishes.

Herb-Infused Vinegar: Make herb-infused vinegar by adding fresh herbs to a bottle of vinegar. Use the flavored vinegar in dressings and marinades.

By incorporating fresh herbs into our cooking and exploring different ways to use them, we not only elevate the taste of our dishes but also enjoy the added nutritional benefits they offer. Herbs are a fantastic way to add variety to our meals while ensuring we get a dose of essential vitamins and minerals as part of our "5 a day" intake.

Chapter 24

Coffee Addicts and Ice Latte Lovers

Believe it or not, coffee beans do contain fiber, whereas freeze-dried coffee loses most of its fiber content during processing. Coffee is also a nerve stimulant and can stay in the system for up to 14 hours. Consider coffee before noon and enjoy after eating food.

Many people are indeed consuming coffee beverages from well-known coffee shops that are loaded with sugary plant milks, syrups, and tempting cakes. Let's look at the sugar content in some common coffee beverages from popular coffee shop chains:

Caramel Macchiato (Grande size): Approximately 32 grams of sugar.
Mocha (Grande size): Approximately 35 grams of sugar.
Iced Vanilla Latte (Grande size): Approximately 27 grams of sugar.
Excessive sugar consumption is a concern for public health as it is linked to various health issues, including obesity, type 2 diabetes, tooth decay, and heart disease. Regularly consuming high-sugar coffee beverages, along with other sugary foods and drinks, can contribute to an overall high intake of added sugars in the diet.

To help you enjoy coffee with lower sugar content, here are ten coffee recipes that are low in sugar and syrups:

Simple Black Coffee: Brew fresh coffee and enjoy it as is, without any added sugar or syrups.

Café Au Lait with Unsweetened Almond Milk: Mix equal parts of brewed coffee and unsweetened almond milk for a creamy and lightly nutty flavor.

Cinnamon Latte: Brew fresh coffee, add a sprinkle of ground cinnamon, and stir. Optionally, use a splash of full-fat milk or unsweetened almond milk.

Coconut Iced Coffee: Brew coffee and let it cool. Mix with coconut milk (canned, not the coconut milk beverage) for a refreshing and tropical taste.

Iced Americano: Brew a double shot of espresso and pour it over ice. Add cold water to your desired strength.

Honey Vanilla Latte: Brew coffee, add a touch of honey and a dash of vanilla extract. Use a splash of full-fat milk or unsweetened almond milk.

Chai Latte with Cinnamon: Brew a chai tea bag in hot water and mix with brewed coffee. Add a sprinkle of ground cinnamon.

Iced Green Tea Latte with Matcha: Brew a strong green tea and mix with a teaspoon of matcha powder. Add a splash of full-fat milk or unsweetened almond milk.

Cold Brew Coffee: Brew coffee using the cold brew method and serve it over ice. Add a splash of full-fat milk or unsweetened almond milk if desired.

By opting for these coffee recipes with lower sugar content and using better alternatives to sugary plant milks and syrups, you can enjoy a healthier coffee experience without compromising on flavor. Make savvy choices when using plant milks, look at the sugar content or better yet make your own.

Chapter 25

Power on Down

Once upon a time in the bustling city of TechTown , there lived a man named Jake. Jake was a charismatic and ambitious fellow, but he had a peculiar addiction that kept him up all night – his beloved iPhone. From the moment he woke up, it was glued to his hand like an extra limb. It became his constant companion, and his life slowly spiraled out of balance.

As days turned into nights, Jake's circadian rhythm went haywire. He would stay up late, scrolling through endless social media feeds, mesmerized by the infinite sea of other people's problems. The constant bombardment of complaints, rants, and drama on social media left him feeling anxious and overwhelmed.

Every morning, as the sun peeked over the horizon, Jake's first instinct was to grab his phone. Little did he know that this habit was setting him up for a rollercoaster of emotions right from the start. The moment he unlocked the screen, a deluge of notifications would flood in, greeting him with news of world crises, friend's heartbreaks, and celebrity scandals.

As Jake's eyes widened, his heart raced, and he couldn't help but feel emotionally tangled in the problems of the world before he even had a chance to sip his morning coffee. It was a maddening whirlpool of information, sucking him deeper into the abyss of social media and making him a slave to the phone.

Sleep became elusive, and Jake found himself tossing and turning in bed, his mind still racing with the worries and issues he encountered online. His days were filled with constant fidgeting and mood swings, as the barrage of news continued to take its toll.

One day, a quirky old man named Mr. Wise, who lived in a quaint little cottage on the outskirts of TechTown , noticed Jake's predicament. Mr. Wise was known for his unconventional wisdom and peculiar remedies for modern-day troubles.

Approaching Jake with a twinkle in his eye, Mr. Wise said, "Ah, young man, it seems you're shackled to that tiny device like a prisoner to his chains. You must learn to break free and find balance in the digital sea."

Intrigued, Jake listened attentively as Mr. Wise shared his pearls of wisdom. He suggested leaving the phone aside for an hour before bedtime, indulging in a good book instead. Mr. Wise recommended taking morning walks without the phone, to allow the mind to breathe and be free from the constant noise.

Jake followed Mr. Wise's advice diligently. He created a bedtime ritual, which included reading a book and sipping herbal tea, and miraculously, sleep started to embrace him warmly once again.

As Jake spent more time away from the phone, he realized that his anxious thoughts began to subside. He found solace in focusing on the present moment and the beauty of the world around him.

And so, the once-addicted Jake slowly but surely reclaimed his life from the clutches of his iPhone. He rediscovered the wonders of true connection, the magic of sleep, and the joy of living without being bombarded by the problems of the world.

From that day forward, whenever Jake found himself slipping back into old habits, he would visit Mr. Wise. The wise old man would always remind him with a chuckle, "Remember, young man, the best connections are the ones made with the heart, not through a screen."

And so, with a laugh and a newfound sense of liberation, Jake embraced a simpler and more fulfilling life, cherishing the charming moments that life had to offer, away from the addictive grasp of his once-beloved iPhone.

Chapter 26

Food and Mood, Your Mental Health

Have you ever considered that the food you eat can greatly influence your emotional well-being? Extensive research has revealed a strong connection between our diet and mental health.

Adopting a nutritious diet can have a positive impact on our mood, reducing stress and increasing energy levels. On the flip side, an unhealthy diet may contribute to mood-related problems like depression, anxiety, and irritability.

Let's delve into the specific ways diet affects our mood:

Nutritional Deficiencies:
When we lack essential nutrients, our mood can suffer. Deficiencies in iron, zinc, B vitamins (especially B6, B9, and B12), magnesium, vitamin D, and omega-3 fatty acids have been linked to mood disorders such as depression and anxiety.
For example:

Insufficient iron levels can lead to fatigue, making it challenging to cope with stress and impacting our mood. Inadequate zinc is associated with depression, anxiety, and irritability as it plays a crucial role in brain function.
B vitamins are integral to various bodily processes, including mood regulation, and low levels of certain B vitamins can lead to depression.
Magnesium is essential for relaxation and sleep, both of which influence our mood. Low magnesium levels have been linked to anxiety and depression.

Inadequate vitamin D, especially during winter months, has been associated with depression.

Blood Sugar Fluctuations:

Fluctuating blood sugar levels can have diverse effects on our mood. Spikes in blood sugar levels can lead to feelings of anxiety, irritability, and difficulty concentrating, while crashes in blood sugar levels can result in fatigue, sadness, and mood swings.

A diet high in processed carbohydrates and sugary foods can cause blood sugar levels to spike and then rapidly drop. In response, the body releases insulin to lower blood sugar levels, which can also contribute to the mentioned symptoms. Recent research suggests that taking a short walk, even just for five minutes after eating, can help manage blood sugar levels and reduce spikes.

Inflammation:

Inflammation is the body's natural response to injury or infection. While it is essential for fighting infections and repairing damage, chronic inflammation can negatively affect our mood.

Processed foods, unhealthy fats (like trans fats and saturated fats), and excessive sugar intake can promote inflammation. These types of foods can damage the gut lining, leading to increased inflammation. Incorporating anti-inflammatory foods rich in omega-3 fatty acids, such as salmon, mackerel, walnuts, flax seeds, and chia seeds, can help balance the omega-3 to omega-6 ratio and reduce inflammation.

The health of our gut is intricately connected to our mental well-being. A healthy gut microbiome produces beneficial chemicals that can improve our mood, while an unhealthy microbiome can produce harmful chemicals that worsen it. The gut microbiome comprises a complex community of bacteria residing in our intestines. These bacteria play a vital role in digestion, nutrient absorption, and immune function. They also produce chemicals like serotonin, dopamine, and GABA (gamma-aminobutyric acid), which influence our mood.

A diet high in processed foods, unhealthy fats, and sugar can disrupt the gut microbiome and lead to inflammation, which, in turn, negatively affects our mood.

Tips for a Mood-Boosting Diet:
To enhance mood and overall well-being, consider incorporating these dietary habits:

Prioritize fruits and vegetables, as they are abundant in vitamins, minerals, and antioxidants that promote a better mood.
Opt for whole grains over processed grains, as they provide sustained energy and help stabilize blood sugar levels.
Include lean protein in your diet to support tissue building and repair, including brain tissue.
Incorporate healthy fats, such as omega-3 fatty acids, to reduce inflammation and foster a positive mood.
Add probiotics to your diet through foods like yogurt or fermented products to support gut health and positively impact mood.

By adopting these healthy dietary choices, you can significantly improve your mood, better manage stress, and boost your energy levels. So, why wait? Take the first step toward a happier, healthier you!

Consuming sugary non-satiety foods can lead to blood glucose fluctuations, which can have significant effects on our moods.

When we eat foods that are high in refined sugars and low in fiber and protein, such as sugary snacks, sweets, and sugary beverages, our blood sugar levels tend to rapidly spike. This is because these foods are quickly digested and absorbed into the bloodstream, causing a sudden surge in blood glucose levels.

When blood sugar levels rise sharply, the body responds by releasing insulin, a hormone that helps transport glucose from the bloodstream into our cells for energy utilization. As a result, blood sugar levels quickly drop after the initial spike, sometimes even lower than before consuming the sugary foods.

This rapid drop in blood sugar is referred to as a "crash," and it can have several negative effects on our mood and well-being:

Feelings of Irritability: A blood sugar crash can trigger feelings of irritability and agitation. The sudden drop in energy levels can leave us feeling moody and impatient.

Fatigue and Lethargy: As blood sugar levels plummet, we may experience a significant decrease in energy, leading to feelings of fatigue and lethargy. This can make it challenging to focus or stay motivated.

Difficulty Concentrating: The fluctuations in blood sugar can impact our cognitive function and ability to concentrate effectively. This can lead to decreased productivity and increased stress.

Emotional Instability: Blood sugar fluctuations can affect the balance of neurotransmitters in the brain, such as serotonin and dopamine, which are closely linked to mood regulation. As a result, we may experience emotional highs and lows.

Increased Cravings: After a blood sugar crash, the body may crave more sugary foods to quickly raise blood glucose levels again, perpetuating a cycle of unhealthy eating habits.

To avoid these mood-altering effects, it's essential to choose foods that have a more gradual impact on blood sugar levels. Opting for whole foods that are rich in fiber, protein, and healthy fats can help stabilize blood sugar levels and provide a more sustained source of energy.

Including foods like whole grains, vegetables, fruits, lean proteins, nuts, and seeds in our diet can contribute to better blood sugar control and a more stable mood throughout the day. Additionally, regular meals and snacks spaced evenly throughout the day can help prevent extreme fluctuations in blood glucose levels.

By being mindful of our food choices and understanding how they impact our blood sugar, we can better support our mood and overall well-being.

Chapter 27

Plant Based Meat Alternatives Good or Bad?

Plant-based meat alternatives have gained immense popularity in recent times due to several factors, including concerns about health, the environment, and animal welfare. These products are specifically designed to replicate the taste, texture, and appearance of conventional meat, all while being made from plant-based ingredients.

But what exactly are meat alternatives? They are food products created from plants, engineered to closely resemble the taste and texture of meat. Common sources for these alternatives include soy, wheat gluten, or pea protein, and they come in various forms such as burgers, sausages, and nuggets. In recent years, the market has expanded to offer plant-based alternatives for bacon, chicken escalope, veggie mince, and even cold cuts like vegan ham and chicken slices, thanks to brands like Quorn.

However, it's essential to consider some drawbacks and factors associated with plant-based meats. While they may offer a healthier option compared to traditional meats, these alternatives still fall under the category of highly processed foods and should be consumed in moderation. Unlike whole foods like vegetables, plant-based meat products contain numerous added ingredients, including higher levels of sodium, saturated fat, and other additives to enhance flavor and texture. In some cases, these products can have as many as 20 different ingredients, raising concerns about their nutritional value.

It's true that the highly processed nature of some plant-based alternatives involves extensive processing to achieve the desired meat-like texture. The manufacturing process can include extrusion, heating, cooling, and the addition of various ingredients. As with any highly processed food, whether plant-based or not, there is a potential for lower nutritional value and the presence of additives or preservatives. Therefore, it's wise to choose plant-based meat alternatives that undergo minimal processing and are made from whole food ingredients whenever possible.

TIP!
"Escape the Calorie Trap: Traditional Diets Miss the Sugar Connection.

These diets often overlook how excessive sugar intake triggers cravings, energy crashes, and overeating."

Chapter 28

The NOVA system

The NOVA system classifies foods into four categories based on their level of processing:

Unprocessed or Minimally Processed Foods: These are foods that undergo little to no processing and are consumed in their natural state or with minimal alterations. Examples include fresh fruits, vegetables, nuts, seeds, and grains.

Processed Culinary Ingredients: This category includes minimally processed foods used in preparing or cooking other dishes, such as oils, butter, sugar, salt, and vinegar.

Processed Foods: Foods in this category have undergone some degree of processing to extend shelf life, enhance taste, or improve convenience. Examples include canned vegetables, fruits in syrup, and freshly made bread.

Ultra-Processed Foods: This category includes foods that have undergone extensive processing and contain numerous additives and artificial substances. These foods are often high in salt, sugar, unhealthy fats, and preservatives. Examples include sugary cereals, packaged snacks, frozen dinners, and many fast-food items.

Understanding the NOVA classification system is essential in comprehending the impact of food processing on nutritional value, health, and dietary patterns. Research has shown that a diet high in ultra-processed foods is associated with an increased risk of obesity, heart disease, and other chronic health conditions. In contrast, diets rich in unprocessed or minimally processed foods tend to be more nutritious and beneficial for overall health.

Given this information, incorporating nutritious plant-based whole foods into our diet can provide essential nutrients and contribute to overall well-being while reducing reliance on highly processed foods, whether they are meat-based or meat alternatives.

Chapter 29

Embrace Food Diversity for Holistic Wellness

Diversifying your diet isn't just about flavors – it's a holistic practice that nurtures your physical, mental, spiritual, nutrient, and biochemical well-being. Just like a symphony of different instruments creates beautiful music, a diverse range of foods enriches your overall health orchestra. Here's why it's so important:

Physical Harmony: A varied diet ensures you get a spectrum of nutrients, supporting different bodily functions and enhancing your physical vitality.

Mental Stimulation: Exploring new foods engages your brain, enhancing cognitive flexibility and creativity, keeping your mind sharp and curious.

Spiritual Connection: Different cuisines can connect you to diverse cultures and traditions, deepening your understanding of the world and fostering a sense of unity.

Nutrient Abundance: Each food offers a unique set of vitamins, minerals, and antioxidants. A diverse diet helps you meet your nutritional needs comprehensively.

Biochemical Resilience: Different foods influence your body's biochemistry in distinct ways. Diversity helps maintain balance and adaptability, contributing to overall health.

Incorporating a variety of foods into your meals is like painting a vibrant canvas of well-being. So, savor the beauty of diversity – on your plate and in your life.

Savvy Bread Recipe!

Here's a recipe for a healthier spelt flour and full-fat Greek yogurt dough that you can use to make a loaf, bread balls, or pizza. I'll also explain why this bread is considered healthier.

Ingredients:

For the Dough:

250g spelt flour
250g full-fat Greek yogurt
1 tsp salt
For the Pizza Topping (you can customize to your liking):

Tomato sauce
Mozzarella cheese
Fresh vegetables (e.g., tomatoes, bell peppers, mushrooms)
Fresh basil leaves
Olive oil
Instructions:

For the Dough:

In a mixing bowl, combine the spelt flour and salt.

Gradually add the full-fat Greek yogurt to the flour mixture, stirring continuously. You may need to use your hands to knead the dough until it becomes smooth and elastic.

Cover the dough with a damp cloth or plastic wrap and let it rest for about 30 minutes. This resting period helps improve the dough's texture.

For the Loaf:

Preheat your oven to 180°C (350°F).

Shape the dough into a loaf and place it on a baking sheet or in a greased loaf tin.

Bake for approximately 25-30 minutes or until the loaf turns golden brown and sounds hollow when tapped on the bottom.

For the Bread Balls:

Preheat your oven to 180°C (350°F).

Divide the dough into small portions and shape them into balls.

Place the dough balls on a baking sheet.

Bake for about 15-20 minutes until they are lightly browned and cooked through.

For the Pizza:

Preheat your oven to its highest temperature (usually around 250-280°C or 480-530°F).

Roll out the dough into the desired pizza shape on a floured surface. You can make one large pizza or several smaller ones.

Place the rolled-out dough on a baking sheet or pizza stone.

Spread a thin layer of tomato sauce over the dough, add your toppings, and finish with a drizzle of olive oil.

Bake in the preheated oven for about 10-15 minutes or until the crust is golden and the cheese is bubbly and slightly browned.

Why This Bread Is Healthier:

Spelt Flour: Spelt flour is a whole grain with a higher protein content and more nutrients than traditional wheat flour. It also tends to be easier to digest for some people.

Full-Fat Greek Yogurt: Full-fat Greek yogurt adds moisture and a creamy texture to the dough while providing protein and healthy fats. It's a better choice than using excessive oil or butter.

No Added Sugar: This recipe doesn't include added sugar, unlike some commercial bread products, making it a healthier choice for those looking to reduce sugar intake.

Customizable Toppings: When making pizza, you have control over the toppings, allowing you to add fresh vegetables and minimize unhealthy options like processed meats or excessive cheese.

This bread offers the benefits of whole grains, healthy fats, and fewer processed ingredients, making it a more nutritious choice for your meals. Enjoy experimenting with different toppings for your pizza!

Chapter 30

Pelvic Floor and Bowl Movement

The pelvic anterior tilt, characterized by an excessive forward tilt of the pelvis, leads to arching of the lower back and protrusion of the abdomen. This posture places increased pressure on the pelvic floor muscles, ligaments, and connective tissues. The pelvic floor provides support to the pelvic organs (bladder, uterus, and rectum) and plays a vital role in controlling urinary and fecal continence. An anterior pelvic tilt can lead to overstretching and weakening of the pelvic floor muscles, resulting in problems like urinary incontinence, pelvic organ prolapse, and pelvic pain.

To support pelvic floor health, locating and maintaining a neutral spine position is crucial. Neutral spine alignment entails minimizing excessive curvature in the lower back. Correctly engaging the pelvic floor muscles within this neutral position can enhance their strength and function. Optimal muscle engagement is achieved when performing pelvic floor exercises like Kegels with a neutral spine, avoiding unnecessary strain.

Diet also impacts pelvic floor health. A diet rich in processed and low-fibre foods can lead to constipation and straining during bowel movements, putting additional pressure on the pelvic floor. A fiber-rich diet and adequate hydration promote regular and softer bowel movements, reducing strain. Avoiding constipation-inducing foods, such as processed items, excessive dairy, and certain medications, also supports healthier bowel habits and minimizes pelvic floor strain.

The pelvic floor consists of muscles forming a supportive sling across the bottom of the pelvis, extending between the pubic bone in front, the tailbone in the back, and the sit bones on each side. It plays essential roles in supporting pelvic organs, maintaining continence, stabilizing the pelvis, and enhancing sexual function. Proper pelvic floor function is essential for overall pelvic health and general well-being.

In conclusion, maintaining a neutral spine posture provides crucial support to the pelvic floor, enhancing its strength and aiding rehabilitation. A fiber-rich diet and avoidance of constipation-inducing foods promote healthier bowel movements, reducing strain on the pelvic floor. Understanding the location and significance of the pelvic floor muscles is vital for maintaining pelvic health and preventing related issues.

Step 1: Prepare for the Alignment:

Stand up straight with your feet hip-width apart, and make sure your weight is evenly distributed between both feet. Allow your arms to relax naturally by your sides.

Step 2: Identify Pelvic Position:

Place your hands on your hip bones (iliac crests) at the front of your pelvis.
Tilt your pelvis forward and backward to feel the extreme positions.

Step 3: Find Neutral Pelvic Position:

Gradually move your pelvis between the forward and backward tilts.
Aim to find the midpoint where your pelvis is in a neutral position, not tilted excessively in either direction.
In the neutral position, your pubic bone and hip bones should form a straight line when viewed from the side.

Step 4: Aligning the Rest of the Spine:

Once you've found neutral pelvis, continue the alignment up your spine.
Make sure your ribcage is not thrust forward or pulled back, but instead, naturally aligned over your pelvis.

Step 5: Head and Neck Alignment:

Align your head and neck in a neutral position. Avoid excessive tilting or bending.
Imagine a straight line extending from the crown of your head down through your spine to your pelvis.

Step 6: Sitting or Lying Down:

You can practice finding neutral spine while sitting or lying down as well.
When sitting, align your pelvis and spine as described above. Use a cushion or back support if needed to maintain the alignment.
When lying down, lie on your back with your knees bent and feet flat on the floor. Follow the steps for pelvic alignment and overall spine alignment.

Step 7: Awareness and Practice:

Be mindful of your posture throughout the day, whether standing, sitting, or lying down.
Regularly practice finding neutral spine to develop muscle memory and reinforce good alignment.
Remember, everyone's body is different, and it may take some time to become accustomed to neutral spine alignment. With practice, you'll develop a better sense of how to maintain this alignment, which can help support your pelvic floor and overall spinal health.

Chapter 31

The Power of Anticipation

the anticipation created by cooking food can aid digestion. When we anticipate a meal that we have cooked ourselves or one that has been prepared with care, our bodies begin to produce more saliva and stomach acid in preparation for digestion. This natural response helps break down the food more efficiently when we finally consume it.

Additionally, the enjoyment and satisfaction derived from a well-cooked meal can have a positive impact on the release of digestive enzymes and hormones, contributing to better digestion. The emotional connection and pleasure associated with the anticipation of a thoughtfully prepared meal can also reduce stress levels, which can further aid digestion.

On the other hand, meals that lack anticipation or are consumed hastily without much thought or appreciation may not trigger the same digestive responses, potentially leading to a less efficient digestion process. Therefore, the anticipation and enjoyment of a carefully cooked meal can indeed aid digestion.

Chapter 32

Toxic People, not everyone is sweet!

we have emphasized the importance of wise choices in managing sugar consumption. Nevertheless, we recognize that true holistic wellness encompasses not only the physical aspect but also our emotional health. Just as eliminating sugar is vital for vitality, bidding farewell to toxic individuals can profoundly empower our mental and emotional well-being.

Understanding Toxic Relationships:

Toxic relationships manifest in various ways, often involving negative, manipulative, or unsupportive individuals that drain our energy and affect our emotional state. The impact of toxic connections can lead to stress, anxiety, and even physical health concerns. Identifying these relationships and acknowledging their detrimental effects is the initial step towards creating positive change.

The Power of Letting Go:

Letting go of toxic relationships is an act of self-preservation and self-love, though admittedly challenging. By doing so, we open ourselves to personal growth and emotional liberation. Breaking free from toxic ties enables us to create space for healthier, more nurturing relationships that support our well-being and aspirations.

Embracing Positive Connections:

As we bid farewell to toxic influences, we create room for positive and uplifting connections that inspire and motivate us. Surrounding ourselves with supportive friends, family, and like-minded individuals fosters a sense of belonging and bolsters our self-esteem. Positive relationships provide a safe space to grow and thrive, offering security and encouragement.

Stress and Mental Health: Toxic relationships often involve conflicts, manipulation, and emotional abuse, leading to chronic stress and negatively impacting mental health. The persistent release of stress hormones weakens the immune system, increases the risk of anxiety and depression, and contributes to various physical health issues.

Self-Esteem and Body Image: Toxic individuals can erode our self-esteem and body image with negative comments and criticism, leading to self-doubt and feelings of inadequacy. Poor body image can disrupt our relationship with food and exercise, hindering physical improvement.

Unhealthy Coping Mechanisms: Faced with challenges in toxic relationships, some resort to unhealthy coping mechanisms like emotional eating, substance abuse, or isolation. These strategies can have detrimental effects on physical health, resulting in weight gain, addiction, and other health problems.

Disrupted Sleep Patterns: Toxic relationships cause worry, anxiety, and emotional turmoil, leading to disrupted sleep patterns. Lack of restorative sleep weakens the immune system, impairs cognitive function, and negatively affects physical well-being.

Physical Health Effects: Chronic stress from toxic relationships contributes to various physical health problems, including cardiovascular issues, gastrointestinal disorders, and weakened immune function. Over time, these consequences take a toll on overall well-being.

Energy Drain: Emotionally draining and exhausting, toxic relationships deplete our energy, leaving little motivation for self-care and physical activities.

Interference with Health Goals: Toxic relationships may hinder adopting a healthy lifestyle. Individuals who don't support health goals discourage exercise, balanced diets, or self-care.

Social Isolation: Toxic relationships lead to social isolation as individuals' distance themselves from supportive friends and family. Social isolation negatively affects mental and physical health, increasing feelings of loneliness and stress.

It is essential to recognize the impact of toxic relationships on our health and take steps to distance ourselves from negativity. Prioritizing positive connections and fostering a supportive environment are vital for achieving holistic well-being and a healthier, happier life.

Catherine's Favourite Self Improvement Books

"These books offer valuable insights, practical advice, and inspiration to support personal growth, emotional well-being, and living a fulfilling life. Whether you're seeking success, happiness, or better relationships, these authors provide valuable tools and perspectives to empower positive change."

"Sane New World: Taming the Mind" - Ruby Wax explores mindfulness and provides practical strategies to manage stress and improve mental well-being.

"A Mindfulness Guide for the Frazzled" - In this book, Ruby Wax shares her personal experiences with mindfulness and offers exercises to cultivate mindfulness in daily life.

"How to Be Human: The Manual" - Co-authored with neuroscientist Ash Ranpura and Buddhist monk Gelong Thubten, this book explores human behavior and emotions, providing insights into improving our lives.

Books by Jay Shetty:

"Think Like a Monk: Train Your Mind for Peace and Purpose Every Day" - Jay Shetty draws from his time as a monk to offer wisdom and guidance on finding purpose and fulfillment.

"Purposeful: Are You a Manager or a Movement Starter?" - In this book, Jay Shetty discusses how to create a meaningful and purpose-driven life and inspire positive change.

"Think Like a Monk Journal: Train Your Mind for Peace and Purpose Every Day" - This journal accompanies Jay Shetty's book, providing practical exercises for self-reflection and personal growth.

"Think Like a Monk Guided Meditation: Train Your Mind for Peace and Purpose Every Day" - Jay Shetty offers guided meditation sessions to enhance mindfulness and focus.

"The 7 Habits of Highly Effective People" by Stephen R. Covey: This classic bestseller offers timeless principles for personal and interpersonal effectiveness to achieve lasting success.

"Big Magic: Creative Living Beyond Fear" by Elizabeth Gilbert: Elizabeth Gilbert encourages readers to embrace their creativity and live a fulfilling life driven by curiosity and passion.

"The Four Agreements" by Don Miguel Ruiz: This insightful book presents four powerful agreements to transform life by embracing personal freedom and happiness.

"The Power of Habit: Why We Do What We Do in Life and Business" by Charles Duhigg: Charles Duhigg explores the science of habit formation and how to create positive habits for success.

"You Are a Badass at Making Money: Master the Mindset of Wealth" by Jen Sincero: Jen Sincero provides practical advice and mindset shifts to overcome limiting beliefs and achieve financial success.

"The Gifts of Imperfection: Let Go of Who You Think You're Supposed to Be and Embrace Who You Are" by Brené Brown: Brené Brown advocates embracing imperfections and cultivating self-acceptance for wholehearted living.

"The Alchemist" by Paulo Coelho: A philosophical novel about following one's dreams and finding purpose and meaning in life's journey.

"The Subtle Art of Not Giving a F*ck: A Counterintuitive Approach to Living a Good Life" by Mark Manson: Mark Manson challenges conventional self-help advice, advocating for embracing life's challenges and choosing what truly matters.

"The 5 Love Languages: The Secret to Love that Lasts" by Gary Chapman: Gary Chapman explores the five love languages and how understanding them can improve relationships and emotional well-being.

A Message from Catherine

Dear readers,

The subject of cancer can be daunting, and I empathize with your fears and concerns. It hits close to home for me as well, as my own mother passed away from cancer, leaving behind a 16-year-old girl, myself. Like many of you, I used to avoid even mentioning the word "cancer" as it felt overwhelming and unsettling.

Over the years, I gently ventured into my own research, trying to understand this complex disease better. Looking back at my mother's dietary habits, I couldn't help but notice how modern-day diets, filled with high sugar content and constant grazing, might have influenced her health.

In response to this realization, I decided to make positive changes in my own life. I embarked on a sugar-free lifestyle, where sugary treats became occasional indulgences. For instance, during my recent trip to Italy, I couldn't resist savoring their delightful gelato and cornetto con crema. These special moments of treating myself have become more meaningful and memorable since they are few and far between.

By adopting a sensible dietary pattern for the majority of the time, I found joy in the occasional treats while ensuring my overall health remained a top priority. I discovered that moderation and mindfulness allow me to enjoy life's pleasures without compromising my well-being.

I share this journey with you because I believe that knowledge and informed choices can be powerful tools in our fight against cancer. We can empower ourselves to make positive changes in our lifestyles and diets to support our health and well-being.

While cancer can be frightening, let us not be paralyzed by fear. Instead, let's arm ourselves with information and take proactive steps to lead healthier lives. By sharing our experiences and knowledge, we create a community of support and understanding that can inspire positive transformations.

Remember, every small change matters, and together, we can embrace hope, resilience, and determination on our path to wellness.

Chapter 33

"Cancer Loves Sugar! So don't feed it."

Cancer cells exhibit a unique characteristic known as increased glucose uptake, meaning they have a higher demand for glucose (sugar) compared to normal cells. This phenomenon, known as the "Warburg effect," was first observed by Nobel Prize-winning scientist Otto Warburg.

Insulin, a hormone produced by the pancreas, plays a critical role in regulating blood sugar levels. When we consume carbohydrates, they are broken down into glucose, which enters the bloodstream. Insulin facilitates the transportation of glucose from the bloodstream into cells, where it can be used as energy or stored for later use.

In certain cancer types, including breast cancer, there is an overexpression of insulin receptors on cancer cells. These receptors are proteins on the cell surface that bind to insulin. The abundance of insulin receptors on cancer cells makes them highly sensitive to insulin in the bloodstream.

When insulin levels are elevated, such as after consuming a carbohydrate-rich meal, it can lead to increased glucose uptake by cancer cells. This provides cancer cells with the energy they need to grow and multiply rapidly. Cancer cells heavily rely on glucose metabolism for their energy needs, making insulin a potential driver of cancer growth.

Furthermore, insulin is known to stimulate the production of insulin-like growth factors (IGFs), which are proteins that promote cell proliferation and survival. Elevated insulin and IGF levels in the bloodstream create a favourable environment for cancer cell growth and survival.

Studies have linked elevated insulin levels to an increased risk of breast cancer development and recurrence. Insulin resistance, a condition where cells become less responsive to insulin's effects, has also been associated with a higher risk of breast cancer.

While insulin and glucose may play a role in cancer development and growth, it's important to understand that cancer is a complex disease influenced by multiple factors, including genetics, lifestyle choices, and environmental factors.

To potentially mitigate the impact of insulin on cancer growth, individuals can consider adopting a balanced and healthful diet that helps maintain stable blood sugar levels. Reducing the consumption of sugary and highly processed foods and incorporating more whole grains, vegetables, and lean proteins can be beneficial. Regular exercise and maintaining a healthy weight are also crucial for overall health and may help support balanced insulin levels.

As always, if there are concerns about health or cancer risk, it is essential to consult with a healthcare professional for personalized advice and guidance. Understanding the complexities of cancer and its relationship with insulin and glucose empowers individuals to make informed decisions about their health and well-being.

In the realm of cancer biology, the rapid growth and multiplication of cancer cells occur due to the disruption of the body's natural regulatory mechanisms controlling cell division. This uncontrolled proliferation leads to the formation of tumors and poses a significant threat to overall health.

Our dietary habits can inadvertently promote cancer cell growth through various means:

Insulin and Growth Promotion: Frequent consumption of excessive food, particularly foods high in sugar and processed carbohydrates, can lead to frequent spikes in insulin levels. As a hormone promoting cell growth, this can inadvertently fuel the growth of cancer cells, which often possess an abundance of insulin receptors, making them more susceptible to its effects.

Inflammation: Diets high in sugar and unhealthy foods can trigger chronic inflammation in the body. This inflammatory environment can support cancer cell growth and progression.

Obesity: Overeating and excessive calorie consumption can lead to weight gain and obesity, which is linked to an increased risk of certain cancers. Additionally, fat cells produce hormones and growth factors that further support cancer cell growth.

The impact of sugar on cancer cell growth is profound because cancer cells have an elevated demand for energy, and they can metabolize sugar at a higher rate than normal cells. By consuming large quantities of sugar, we inadvertently provide cancer cells with the energy needed to multiply and thrive.

In the battle against cancer, there are three primary approaches:

Radiation Therapy: This treatment method involves utilizing high-energy beams to target and destroy cancer cells. The radiation damages the DNA within cancer cells, inhibiting their ability to divide and grow.

Chemotherapy: Chemotherapy employs drugs that specifically target rapidly dividing cells, including cancer cells. Administered either orally or intravenously, these drugs circulate throughout the body to seek and destroy cancer cells wherever they may be.

Surgery: In certain cases, surgical intervention may be necessary to remove cancerous tumors or affected tissues from the body.

Intermittent fasting shows promise in slowing down cancer cell growth due to several mechanisms:

Reduced Insulin Levels: Fasting periods lead to decreased insulin levels, starving cancer cells that are sensitive to insulin's growth-promoting effects.

Autophagy: During fasting, the process of autophagy is triggered, wherein cells recycle damaged components. This self-renewal process can help remove faulty cellular material and contribute to slowing cancer cell growth.

Enhanced Immune Response: Intermittent fasting has been observed to boost the immune system's capacity to target and eliminate cancer cells, aiding in the body's defense against cancer progression.

Regarding certain groups, like the Inuit's, having lower cancer rates due to their environment, it is believed that their traditional diet, rich in natural foods like fish, plays a role in protecting against cancer. However, when these populations adopt a Westernized diet with increased consumption of processed and sugary foods, their cancer rates may rise, illustrating the profound influence of diet and lifestyle on cancer risk.

In conclusion, understanding the impact of our dietary choices and lifestyle on cancer growth can empower us to make informed decisions to promote overall health and wellbeing. It is essential to recognize that cancer is a complex disease influenced by various factors, and early detection, personalized treatment, and continued medical care are vital aspects in managing cancer effectively.

Indigenous Amazonian Tribes: Certain indigenous tribes in the Amazon rainforest, like the Tsimane people of Bolivia, have been found to have relatively low incidences of cancer. Their traditional lifestyle involves a diet rich in wild game, fish, fruits, and vegetables, and they engage in regular physical activity. Their diet is generally low in processed foods and high in natural antioxidants, which may offer protective effects against cancer.

Okinawans (Japan): The Okinawan people of Japan have long been recognized for their longevity and relatively low rates of cancer. Their diet consists of nutrient-dense, plant-based foods with a focus on vegetables, sweet potatoes, tofu, and fish. They also practice "Hara Hachi Bu," a cultural practice of eating until they are 80% full, which helps in maintaining a healthy weight and potentially reduces cancer risk.

Maasai (Tanzania and Kenya): The Maasai tribe in East Africa has been found to have lower rates of certain cancers. Their traditional diet consists mainly of milk, meat, and blood from cattle. They also have an active lifestyle, which may contribute to their reduced cancer risk.

Inuit (Arctic Regions): The Inuit people living in Arctic regions have historically had lower cancer rates. Their traditional diet, known as the "Inuit Paradox," is high in fat and protein from fish, marine mammals, and other wild game. However, modern dietary changes and the adoption of Westernized diets have been associated with an increase in cancer incidence among some Inuit populations.

While these observations suggest a potential link between lifestyle, diet, and lower cancer rates, it's important to note that cancer is a complex disease influenced by multiple factors, including genetics, environmental exposures, and access to healthcare. The lifestyle and dietary practices of these populations may contribute to their relatively lower cancer rates, but more research is needed to fully understand the underlying mechanisms and potential implications for cancer prevention and treatment.

Dr. Jason Fung, a renowned authority on fasting and intermittent fasting, has written a book titled "The Complete Guide to Fasting: Heal Your Body Through Intermittent, Alternate-Day, and Extended Fasting." In this book, he delves into the numerous benefits and practical applications of fasting to promote overall health and well-being.

More about Intermittent Fasting

Intermittent fasting is an eating pattern that alternates between eating and fasting periods, focusing on when to eat rather than what to eat. Methods include the 16/8 (16 hours fasting, 8-hour eating window) and 5:2 (normal eating 5 days, low calorie 2 days). It offers benefits such as lowered insulin levels, promoting fat utilization and metabolic health, and triggering autophagy for cellular repair and longevity. Improved hormone regulation and brain function are observed, and it simplifies eating patterns, encouraging healthier food choices.

For beginners, seeking guidance from healthcare professionals or dietitians is crucial to ensure safe implementation. Aiming for a 12-hour fasting period from dinner to breakfast allows the body to repair, optimize hormones, and lower insulin, contributing to overall well-being.

Those struggling with fasting may have nutrient-deficient diets, leading to insufficient satiety during fasting periods. Balancing meals with protein, healthy fats, and fiber-rich foods can sustain energy levels and reduce hunger.

According to the insights shared by Dr. Jason Fung, a prominent authority on intermittent fasting and nutrition, fasting offers a unique opportunity for the body to undergo a natural process known as autophagy. Autophagy is the body's way of self-cleaning and repairing, involving the removal of damaged cellular components, such as proteins and organelles.

During fasting, the body experiences reduced levels of insulin and glucose, prompting a shift from relying on glucose for energy to utilizing stored fat. This metabolic shift enhances insulin sensitivity in the cells, which is favourable for overall health. By abstaining from constant food intake during fasting, the body prioritizes repair and rejuvenation over cell growth and replication.

Avoiding the promotion of continuous cell growth is particularly relevant when considering cancer development. Cancer cells, like all cells, thrive on glucose as their primary energy source. Elevated insulin and glucose levels can foster cell growth, including cancer cell proliferation. Hence, excessive consumption of sugar and refined carbohydrates, which stimulate constant cell growth, might increase the risk of cancer or exacerbate its progression.

Embracing intermittent fasting allows the body to enter periods of rest from constant nutrient intake, enabling it to focus on essential self-cleaning and healing processes. By integrating intermittent fasting into our routines, we provide our bodies with valuable opportunities to optimize health, enhance insulin sensitivity, and potentially reduce the likelihood of chronic diseases, including cancer.

My Top 5 Books on Intermittent Fasting:

"The Obesity Code: Unlocking the Secrets of Weight Loss" by Dr. Jason Fung.

"Delay, Don't Deny: Living an Intermittent Fasting Lifestyle" by Gin Stephens.

"The Complete Guide to Fasting: Heal Your Body Through Intermittent, Alternate-Day, and Extended Fasting" by Dr. Jason Fung and Jimmy Moore.

"The Fast Diet: The Simple Secret of Intermittent Fasting" by Dr. Michael Mosley and Mimi Spencer.

"Intermittent Fasting For Women: The Complete Beginners Guide for Weight Loss, Burn Fat, Heal Your Body Through The Self-Cleansing Process of Autophagy and Live a Healthy Lifestyle" by Sarah Amber Patterson.

These books offer valuable insights and practical strategies for those interested in exploring intermittent fasting for improved health and well-being.

Chapter 34

Barefoot Sugar Savvy Squad

"You always know when someone has been talking to Catherine, because they're now on a low sugar diet, have switched to rye sour dough bread and wear barefoot trainers!"

Advocated by experts and enthusiasts, going barefoot and wearing minimalist trainers offer numerous benefits for posture, foot strength, and overall foot health. Some key advantages include:

Natural Foot Movement: Going barefoot allows for unrestricted foot movement, promoting a more natural gait, better posture, and reduced risk of movement imbalances and foot issues.

Strengthening Foot Muscles: Barefoot shoes challenge foot muscles, leading to increased strength and flexibility compared to traditional shoes that often provide excessive support.

Improved Proprioception: Barefoot walking or minimalist shoes enhance proprioception, providing more sensory feedback to the brain, resulting in improved balance and coordination.

Reduced Impact Forces: Advocates claim that barefoot or minimalist footwear can lessen impact forces during walking or running, leading to less stress on joints.

Correcting Posture and Alignment: Allowing feet to function naturally may contribute to better overall alignment and posture by avoiding alterations caused by cushioned and supportive shoes.

Preventing Foot Problems: Switching to minimalist footwear or going barefoot may help prevent or alleviate foot conditions like bunions, hammer toes, and plantar fasciitis by promoting proper foot mechanics.

It is important to note that transitioning to barefoot or minimalist footwear should be gradual, considering individual foot anatomy, lifestyle, and existing foot conditions. Consulting with a podiatrist or foot health specialist before making significant changes is wise to ensure personalized advice and a smooth transition towards better foot health.

Popular Barefoot Shoe Companies:

Vibram FiveFingers
Vivobarefoot
Xero Shoes
Saguaro
Merrell Barefoot
Lems Shoes
Earth Runners
Feelgrounds
Tadeevo
Freet Footwear
Unshoes

Please remember to research and try out different brands to find the barefoot shoe that best suits your needs and preferences.

Chapter 35

Nasal Breathing

James Nestor's "Breath: The New Science of a Lost Art" is a captivating exploration of the power of conscious breathing on our health. Through scientific research and historical insights, Nestor uncovers the impact of modern lifestyle on our breathing patterns. He reveals how inefficient breathing affects sleep, anxiety, and overall well-being. The book offers transformative breathing techniques like the Buteyko Method to improve oxygen uptake and reduce stress. Nestor's engaging storytelling and empowering insights make "Breath" a must-read for those curious about the profound effects of something as simple as our breath on our physical and mental health.

"It's one of my favourite books!" - Catherine

Nasal breathing offers numerous benefits for our overall health and well-being. Here are some compelling reasons why we should prioritize nasal breathing:

Air Filtration: The nasal passages act as a natural filter, removing dust, allergens, and pathogens from the air we breathe, promoting cleaner and healthier air intake.

Humidification: Nasal breathing adds moisture to the inhaled air, preventing the respiratory system from drying out and reducing the risk of irritation or discomfort.

Nitric Oxide Production: The nasal sinuses produce nitric oxide, a gas with various health benefits, including antimicrobial properties, improved blood flow, and immune system support.

Enhanced Oxygen Uptake: Nitric oxide produced during nasal breathing helps increase oxygen uptake in the lungs and improves oxygen delivery to cells, supporting better overall oxygenation.

Improved Lung Function: Nasal breathing regulates the volume of air inhaled, preventing over-breathing and optimizing oxygen-carbon dioxide exchange in the lungs.

Calming Effect on Nervous System: Nasal breathing activates the parasympathetic nervous system, promoting relaxation, reducing stress, and enhancing overall mental well-being.

Reduced Risk of Infections: The air-filtering capacity of the nasal passages helps reduce the risk of respiratory infections and allergies by trapping pathogens before they reach the lungs.

Optimal Breathing Rhythm: Nasal breathing encourages a slower, more controlled breathing pattern, promoting better control of breathing rate and depth.

Energy Conservation: Nasal breathing helps conserve energy during rest and light activities by optimizing oxygen uptake and carbon dioxide elimination.

Mind-Body Connection: Focusing on nasal breathing can enhance mindfulness, allowing us to be more present in the moment and better connected to our bodies and surroundings.

By prioritizing nasal breathing and making it a regular part of our daily life, we can unlock its remarkable health benefits and enhance our overall physical, mental, and emotional well-being.

TIP!
"Expose mushrooms to sunlight for 30 minutes before consumption to enhance their nutritional value. Sunlight triggers vitamin D production in mushrooms, promoting bone health and immunity. This easy step adds a natural boost to their benefits, improving taste and overall wellness."

Chapter 36

Sunlight and Movement

Sunlight is an essential natural resource that provides numerous benefits for our overall health and well-being. Here are some key reasons why we need sunlight and why going outside to move is crucial, backed by science:

Vitamin D Production: Sunlight is a vital source of vitamin D, which plays a crucial role in bone health, immune function, and overall well-being. When our skin is exposed to sunlight, it synthesizes vitamin D, promoting its essential functions in the body.

Mood Enhancement: Sunlight exposure triggers the release of serotonin, a neurotransmitter associated with mood regulation and feelings of happiness and well-being. Spending time outdoors in the sunlight can help improve mood and reduce symptoms of depression and anxiety.

Circadian Rhythm Regulation: Exposure to natural light, especially in the morning, helps regulate our circadian rhythm, the internal body clock that controls sleep-wake cycles. Proper circadian rhythm alignment enhances sleep quality and overall energy levels.

Melatonin Balance: Sunlight exposure during the day helps regulate melatonin production, a hormone that plays a role in sleep-wake cycles. Balanced melatonin levels contribute to better sleep patterns.

Bone Health: Sunlight is crucial for calcium absorption and bone health. Adequate vitamin D levels, obtained through sunlight exposure, support bone development and reduce the risk of bone-related disorders.

Immune System Support: Sunlight exposure has been linked to a stronger immune system, with some studies suggesting that sunlight's effects on T-cells and white blood cells can enhance immune response.

Physical Activity: Going outside encourages physical activity, whether it's walking, jogging, cycling, or engaging in recreational sports. Regular movement is essential for cardiovascular health, muscle strength, and overall fitness.

Mental Refreshment: Spending time outdoors and moving in nature can offer mental rejuvenation and reduce feelings of stress and mental fatigue.

Eye Health: Sunlight exposure is associated with a lower risk of myopia (nearsightedness) in children and can support overall eye health.

Seasonal Affective Disorder (SAD): Sunlight exposure is known to alleviate symptoms of Seasonal Affective Disorder, a type of depression linked to changes in seasons, particularly in regions with reduced sunlight during certain times of the year.

Chapter 37

The Nutritious Rainbow Diet Pattern

The "Eat the Rainbow" diet pattern is not only visually appealing but also a highly nutritious approach to eating. By incorporating a wide array of colorful fruits, vegetables, and other whole foods, this diet provides a diverse range of vitamins, minerals, antioxidants, and phytochemicals that are essential for overall health. Each vibrant color in the rainbow signifies different nutrients and health benefits, making this eating style a delicious and wholesome way to nourish our bodies.

Starting with Dinner for Breakfast: Satiety Throughout the Day

In this unique meal plan, we encourage starting the day with a more substantial dinner-like meal and gradually transitioning to lighter options for dinner. This approach helps provide lasting satiety throughout the day, supporting stable energy levels and reducing the likelihood of overeating later in the evening. The nutrient-dense dinners for breakfast also offer a powerful kickstart to the day, providing essential nutrients and promoting a sense of fullness that can carry you through until lunchtime.

Tips for Meal Prepping and Planning

Create a Colorful Grocery List: Plan your meals around different colors of fruits, vegetables, and protein sources to ensure a balanced and diverse diet.

Prep Ahead: On weekends or your free days, chop vegetables, cook grains, and pre-cook proteins to have them readily available during the week.

Batch Cooking: Prepare larger quantities of certain dishes, like soups or stews, and freeze them in individual portions for quick and easy meals.

Mason Jar Salads: Layer your salads in mason jars, starting with dressing at the bottom and adding denser ingredients towards the top. When ready to eat, shake the jar and enjoy!

Smoothie Packs: Pre-portion smoothie ingredients in ziplock bags or containers, so all you have to do is add liquid and blend in the morning.

Keep Healthy Snacks on Hand: Prepare snack-sized portions of nuts, seeds, and cut fruits to have nutritious snacks readily available.

Stay Hydrated: Don't forget to drink plenty of water throughout the day to support digestion and overall well-being.

By following the "Eat the Rainbow" meal plan and adopting smart meal prepping strategies, you can not only enjoy delicious and satisfying meals but also nourish your body with a wide range of nutrients for optimal health.

Day 1: Red

Breakfast: Baked salmon with a side of roasted beets and steamed broccoli.
Lunch: Grilled chicken salad with mixed greens, cherry tomatoes, red bell peppers, and olive oil dressing.
Dinner: Tomato, spinach, and mushroom omelet with avocado slices.

Day 2: Orange

Breakfast: Grilled chicken with roasted sweet potatoes and sautéed kale.
Lunch: Spicy shrimp and avocado salad with orange segments and a lemon vinaigrette.
Dinner: Scrambled eggs with sautéed spinach, carrots, and a side of mixed berries.

Day 3: Yellow

Breakfast: Baked cod with a side of steamed yellow squash and zucchini.
Lunch: Grilled lemon herb chicken with cauliflower rice and yellow bell peppers.
Dinner: Banana and coconut milk smoothie bowl topped with chia seeds and unsweetened shredded coconut.

Day 4: Green

Breakfast: Zucchini noodles with pesto sauce and grilled shrimp.
Lunch: Avocado and tuna salad with mixed greens and a lime vinaigrette.
Dinner: Green smoothie with spinach, kiwi, cucumber, and a handful of almonds.

Day 5: Blue

Breakfast: Baked salmon with a side of steamed asparagus and a mixed greens salad.
Lunch: Grilled chicken with a side of blue corn tortilla chips, guacamole, and salsa.
Dinner: Blueberry and almond milk chia pudding topped with crushed almonds.

Day 6: Indigo

Breakfast: Mixed berry smoothie with blackberries, raspberries, and strawberries, topped with a dollop of coconut yogurt.
Lunch: Grilled eggplant and portobello mushroom stack with a side of mixed greens.
Dinner: Mixed berry compote with coconut milk and crushed walnuts.

Day 7: Violet

Breakfast: Quinoa salad with roasted beets, purple onions, and a lemon-tahini dressing.

Lunch: Grilled steak with a side of sautéed Swiss chard and rainbow cauliflower.

Dinner: Acai berry bowl with purple grapes, coconut flakes, and a dollop of Greek yogurt.

Chapter 38

Menacing Menopause

Menopause symptoms can be challenging due to hormonal fluctuations and changes in estrogen levels. Hot flashes are believed to occur when there is a sudden drop in estrogen, leading to a disruption in the body's temperature regulation. As a result, blood vessels near the skin's surface dilate, causing a sudden heat sensation and sweating.

The severity of menopause symptoms varies for each woman and is influenced by factors like genetics, lifestyle, and overall health. Hormonal imbalances during menopause can lead to mood swings, irritability, hot flashes, night sweats, and changes in menstrual cycles. The symptoms are often exacerbated by stress, lack of sleep, and unhealthy dietary choices.

Menopause marks a significant transition in a woman's life, and the body is adapting to a new hormonal balance. While the symptoms can be challenging, they are a natural part of the aging process. Managing menopause effectively involves a holistic approach, including diet, exercise, stress management, and seeking professional guidance when necessary. Remember that every woman's menopause journey is unique, and finding individualized strategies to cope with symptoms is essential for overall well-being.

I have Top Tips to Help!

Lower sugar intake: Stabilizes blood sugar levels and reduces hot flashes.

Start the day with savory foods: Helps balance hormones and metabolism. Avoid cereal, skimmed milk, sugar, juices, baked goods, and honey, sweet teas, hot chocolate, juices and sugary smoothies. Go for eggs, Avocadoes, oily fish, veggies, full Greek yogurt bowls, nuts, and seeds, a "healthy" fry up is one of my favourites.

Engage in resistance training: Supports hormone balance, muscle maintenance, and bone health.

Apply Anna's yam: Believed to provide natural relief from menopause symptoms. Available on Amazon and online.

Include phytoestrogen-rich foods: May help regulate estrogen levels and alleviate symptoms.

Manage stress through relaxation techniques: Reduces mood swings and anxiety.

Prioritize sleep: Improves overall well-being and reduces night sweats.

Maintain a healthy weight: Reduces the risk of obesity-related symptoms.

Consume calcium-rich foods: Supports bone health during menopause.

Ensure adequate vitamin D intake: Important for bone health and immune function.

Incorporate omega-3 fatty acids: May help reduce inflammation and support heart health.

Include probiotics in the diet: Supports gut health and may alleviate digestive issues.

Seek support from a community: Provides emotional support and helpful coping strategies.

Use cold compresses or ice packs: Instant relief for hot flashes.

Explore acupuncture or acupressure: May help manage menopause symptoms.

Engage in regular aerobic exercise: Boosts mood and reduces anxiety.

Practice mindfulness techniques: Manage mood changes and enhance well-being.

Enjoy herbal teas like chamomile or peppermint: Known for their calming properties.

Consider cognitive-behavioral therapy (CBT): Helps manage mood changes and anxiety.

Incorporate strength exercises: Pushing and pulling weights maintains muscle mass, supports bone health, and improves overall strength.

Balance estrogen levels with phytoestrogen-rich foods: May help reduce symptoms.

Wear comfortable clothing: Minimizes discomfort during menopause.

Consume magnesium-rich foods: Helps reduce muscle cramps.

Prioritize self-care and hobbies: Promotes relaxation and well-being.

Use cold pillows or fans: Alleviates night sweats.

Practice mindfulness techniques for anxiety: Promotes emotional well-being.

Explore herbal teas or natural supplements for better sleep: May aid in improving sleep quality.

Maintain a balanced diet with nutrient-dense choices: Supports overall health.

Limit triggers like spicy foods, caffeine, or alcohol: Improves sleep quality and symptom management.

Recognize menopause as a natural process: Seeking professional guidance fosters understanding and support.

Care for bone health: Reduces the risk of fractures and osteoporosis.

Stay hydrated: Essential for overall well-being.

Include probiotics in the diet: Supports gut health and immune function.

Engage in gentle stretching exercises like yoga: Improves flexibility and reduces stress.

Keep a symptom diary: Helps identify triggers and manage symptoms.

Maintain a cool and dark bedroom: Improves sleep quality.

Engage in creative activities: Promotes relaxation and self-expression.

If possible, avoid snacking which causes little fires inside the body and insulin spikes. Try to eat meals that will stick around and keep you going for hours.

Prioritize gut health: Supports overall well-being and symptom management.

Consider herbal remedies like black cohosh or red clover: May provide relief for some women.

Limit caffeine and alcohol intake: Helps reduce hot flashes and improves sleep.

Recognize the uniqueness of each woman's menopause journey: Fosters personalized care.

Practice pelvic floor exercises: Promotes bladder control and pelvic health.

Embrace a positive attitude and lifestyle change: Improves the menopause experience.

Balance physical activity and rest: Supports overall health and well-being during menopause.

Maintain social connections: Reduces feelings of isolation and supports mental health.

Incorporate relaxation techniques in daily routines: Reduces stress and anxiety.

Understand hormonal changes during menopause: Fosters self-compassion and informed decisions.

Emphasize nutrient-dense foods: Provides essential vitamins and minerals for overall health.

Drink plenty of water throughout the day.

Including resistance training with weights helps women maintain muscle mass, supports bone health, and enhances overall strength. This is especially important during menopause, as estrogen levels decline, which can lead to muscle loss and decreased bone density. Engaging in resistance training with weights helps counteract these changes and promotes better physical health and function.

Join a gym and speak to a friendly fitness professional, who can write you a basic resistance program, or join in with a group exercise session that includes weights and resistance work.

Davina McCall, a well-known television presenter and personality, has been an influential voice in breaking the silence around menopause. While she may not have authored a specific book dedicated to menopause, her candid and open discussions about her own experience have made a significant impact on women facing the same life transition.

Through various media interviews and personal stories, Davina has fearlessly shared her journey through menopause, shedding light on the challenges and triumphs that come with this natural phase of life. Her relatable and honest approach has resonated with countless women who find comfort and understanding in her words.

Davina's advocacy for menopause awareness has sparked conversations and encouraged women to seek support and education about their own menopausal experiences. By speaking openly about her symptoms, emotions, and coping mechanisms, she has empowered women to navigate this transformative phase with greater confidence and self-awareness.

In the absence of a dedicated book, Davina's willingness to share her menopause journey through interviews and articles serves as a valuable resource for those seeking a relatable perspective. Her candid insights offer reassurance, understanding, and a sense of camaraderie, allowing women to feel less alone in their menopausal struggles and triumphs.

As a prominent figure in the public eye, Davina's openness about menopause has played a crucial role in dispelling myths and reducing the stigma surrounding this natural life stage. Her advocacy has encouraged a more open and supportive dialogue about menopause, creating a safe space for women to discuss their experiences and seek the guidance they need.

In summary, while Davina McCall may not have authored a book specifically on menopause, her advocacy, authenticity, and willingness to share her journey have been instrumental in raising awareness and providing much-needed support for women navigating the menopausal transition. Her contributions have undoubtedly been a source of inspiration and encouragement for countless women facing this transformative phase of life.

Chapter 39

Spice World

Herbs and spices have been cherished for centuries, not just for their ability to tantalize our taste buds, but also for their extraordinary health benefits. These natural gems are abundant in antioxidants, vitamins, and minerals, which fortify our immune system, aid digestion, and enhance overall well-being.

The vibrant golden hue of turmeric brings forth the powerful compound curcumin, celebrated for its anti-inflammatory prowess. On the other hand, the invigorating aroma of basil works wonders in promoting relaxation and easing stress.

Beyond their delightful flavours, these culinary wonders hold ancient healing wisdom passed down through traditional medicine practices. The ingenious pairing of black pepper with turmeric showcases nature's brilliance, creating a synergy that enhances curcumin's absorption and magnifies its potential health advantages.

When we embrace the magic of herbs and spices in our culinary endeavors, we infuse depth and character into our dishes while empowering ourselves to craft nourishing meals without relying on excessive salt, sugar, or unhealthy fats. The delightful harmony of a lemon-herb dressing or the comforting warmth of a cinnamon-spiced dessert exemplifies the artistry of blending flavours that awaken our palates and nurture our bodies.

As we embark on this journey, we celebrate the timeless wisdom of herbs and spices, inspiring us to elevate our cooking and enrich our well-being. Let the natural wonders of these botanical treasures guide us in creating extraordinary feasts that not only delight our senses but also nourish our bodies and spirits.

The notion of "most powerful" herbs and spices varies based on the specific health benefits sought. Nonetheless, certain herbs and spices have garnered recognition for their potential health-promoting properties. Here, we present a compilation of ten widely acclaimed herbs and spices known for their potential benefits:

Turmeric: Boasting curcumin, a potent anti-inflammatory and antioxidant compound, turmeric has been studied for its potential in reducing inflammation, supporting joint health, and enhancing overall well-being.

Ginger: Renowned for its anti-inflammatory properties and digestive benefits, ginger may help alleviate nausea, improve digestion, and fortify the immune system.

Garlic: Containing allicin, a compound with potential antimicrobial and heart health benefits, garlic has been linked to reducing blood pressure, cholesterol levels, and supporting immune function.

Cinnamon: With antioxidant properties, cinnamon may aid in regulating blood sugar levels and has been studied for its potential to enhance insulin sensitivity and support metabolic health.

Ashwagandha: An adaptogenic herb embraced in traditional Ayurvedic medicine, ashwagandha is associated with stress reduction, relaxation promotion, and adrenal health support.

Green Tea: Abundant in antioxidants, green tea may offer support for heart health and metabolism.

Holy Basil (Tulsi): Revered for its adaptogenic properties, holy basil has been linked to potential stress-relieving benefits.

Rosemary: Packed with rosmarinic acid, an antioxidant that may bolster brain health and memory.

Oregano: With powerful compounds possessing potential antimicrobial properties, oregano is a valuable addition to one's culinary repertoire.

Peppermint: Known to aid digestion, reduce bloating, and alleviate headaches, peppermint offers a refreshing and soothing touch.

It is essential to remember that while these herbs and spices have been studied for their potential health advantages, they should not replace professional medical advice or treatment. If incorporating these botanicals into one's diet for specific health concerns, consulting with a healthcare professional is vital to ensure safety and appropriateness for individual needs.

Turmeric and Sumac Roasted Cauliflower:
Ingredients: 500g cauliflower florets, 1 teaspoon turmeric, 1 teaspoon sumac, 2 tablespoons olive oil, 1/2 teaspoon garlic powder, sea salt, and black pepper.

Garlic and Herb Baked Salmon with Turmeric and Sumac:
Ingredients: 4 fresh salmon fillets (about 150g each), 2 cloves of garlic (minced), 1 teaspoon rosemary, 1 teaspoon thyme, juice of 1 lemon, 2 tablespoons olive oil, 1/2 teaspoon turmeric, 1/2 teaspoon sumac, sea salt, and black pepper.

Cinnamon-Sumac Roasted Butternut Squash:
Ingredients: 500g butternut squash cubes, 1 teaspoon cinnamon, 1 teaspoon sumac, 2 tablespoons olive oil, and a sprinkle of sea salt.

Ashwagandha-infused Green Smoothie with Turmeric:
Ingredients: Handful of spinach, handful of kale, 1 cucumber, 1 green apple, 250ml coconut water, thumb-sized piece of fresh ginger, 1/2 teaspoon ashwagandha powder, 1/2 teaspoon turmeric, a pinch of black pepper, and ice.

Lemon-Garlic Grilled Shrimp Skewers with Sumac:
Ingredients: 500g large shrimp, juice of 1 lemon, 2 cloves of garlic (minced), handful of fresh parsley (chopped), 2 tablespoons olive oil, 1 teaspoon sumac, a pinch of black pepper, and wooden skewers.

Rosemary and Sumac Roasted Chicken Thighs:
Ingredients: 4 chicken thighs, 1 teaspoon dried rosemary,
1/2 teaspoon garlic powder, 1/2 teaspoon onion powder,
zest of 1 lemon, 2 tablespoons olive oil, 1 teaspoon sumac,
a pinch of black pepper, and sea salt.

Oregano and Tomato Stuffed Bell Peppers with Turmeric:
Ingredients: 4 bell peppers, 400g lean ground turkey, 400g
diced tomatoes, 1 teaspoon dried oregano, 1 teaspoon dried
basil, 2 cloves of garlic (minced), 1 small onion (diced),
1/2 teaspoon turmeric, 1/2 teaspoon sumac, a sprinkle of
black pepper, and a sprinkle of mozzarella cheese.

Peppermint Chocolate Avocado Mousse with Sumac:
Ingredients: 2 ripe avocados, 2 tablespoons unsweetened
cocoa powder, 250ml almond milk, 1/2 teaspoon
peppermint extract, 1/2 teaspoon sumac, a pinch of black
pepper, and a natural sweetener like stevia or monk fruit
(to taste).

Turmeric and Ginger Chicken Soup with Sumac:
Ingredients: 2 chicken breasts, 1 teaspoon turmeric, thumb-
sized piece of fresh ginger (minced), 2 cloves of garlic
(minced), 2 carrots (sliced), 2 celery sticks (sliced),
handful of spinach, 1 liter chicken broth, 1/2 teaspoon
sumac, a pinch of black pepper, and 250ml coconut milk.

Cinnamon-Sumac Chia Seed Pudding:
Ingredients: 4 tablespoons chia seeds, 500ml almond milk,
1 teaspoon ground cinnamon, 1 teaspoon sumac, a pinch of
black pepper, 1 teaspoon vanilla extract, and a touch of
natural sweetener (optional).
**Enjoy these delicious and healthy recipes with the
added benefits of powerful herbs and spices!**

Chapter 40

Meat

Processed meat is often cheap and unhealthy due to several reasons. Firstly, it is usually made from low-quality cuts of meat that are mechanically processed to add flavorings, preservatives, and other additives. These additives may include high amounts of salt, nitrates, and other chemicals that can have adverse effects on health when consumed in excess.

Additionally, the production process of processed meat involves methods such as smoking, curing, and fermentation, which can create harmful compounds like polycyclic aromatic hydrocarbons (PAHs) and heterocyclic amines (HCAs). These compounds have been associated with an increased risk of certain cancers and other health issues.

Moreover, processed meats are often high in saturated fats and cholesterol, which can contribute to heart disease and other cardiovascular problems. Regular consumption of processed meat has been linked to a higher risk of obesity, diabetes, and other chronic diseases.

Meat is a significant source of essential nutrients like protein, iron, zinc, and vitamin B12, which play crucial roles in various bodily functions. When eliminating meat from the diet, it is essential to find suitable replacements to ensure the body receives these nutrients in adequate amounts.

A vegan or vegetarian diet requires careful consideration and knowledge of how to maintain a balanced intake of nutrients. Simply removing meat without proper substitutes can lead to deficiencies, such as protein deficiency, iron deficiency anemia, and vitamin B12 deficiency, which can have severe health consequences.

Seeking guidance from a qualified nutritionist, dietitian, or healthcare professional is essential before transitioning to a vegan or vegetarian diet. These experts can help design a well-planned diet that meets individual nutritional needs, ensuring that all essential nutrients are adequately supplied through plant-based sources or supplements, if necessary.

A balanced vegan or vegetarian diet should include a wide variety of plant-based foods, such as legumes, nuts, seeds, whole grains, fruits, and vegetables, to provide essential nutrients. Fortified foods or supplements can also be used to ensure an adequate intake of nutrients like vitamin B12, which is primarily found in animal products.

It's crucial to recognize that adopting a vegan or vegetarian diet is a serious decision that requires careful consideration and proper guidance. While it can be a positive step towards ethical and environmental concerns, it is essential to prioritize personal health and well-being by making informed choices about nutrition and seeking professional advice when needed. This way, individuals can confidently embrace a plant-based lifestyle while safeguarding their health and nutritional needs.

Absolutely! Including how to get multiple meals from a roast chicken and indulging in occasional high-quality steak while incorporating more plant-based and vegetarian options can significantly improve overall health and budget. Here are some additional tips:

Roast Chicken Magic: A roast chicken can provide several meals. Enjoy it freshly roasted with vegetables one night, then use the leftover meat for chicken sandwiches or salads the next day. Boil the chicken bones to make a nourishing homemade broth, which can be the base for a comforting chicken soup or stew.

Opt for Quality Steak: Occasionally treat yourself to a high-quality steak from a local butcher or reputable source. By choosing premium cuts less frequently, you can savor the experience while keeping costs manageable.

Embrace Plant-Based Meals: Incorporate more plant-based and vegetarian dishes into your weekly menu. Legumes, tofu, tempeh, and whole grains can be excellent protein sources that are budget-friendly and provide a variety of nutrients.

Bulk Up with Beans and Lentils: Beans and lentils are not only nutritious but also affordable. Use them as the main ingredient in stews, soups, and curries to create hearty and satisfying meals.

Get Creative with Vegetables: Explore different cooking techniques and seasonings to make vegetables the star of the dish. Roasting, grilling, and stir-frying can enhance flavours and textures.

Make Grain Bowls: Build nourishing grain bowls with a variety of cooked grains, roasted vegetables, and protein sources like chickpeas or quinoa. Drizzle with flavorful dressings or sauces for a satisfying and colorful meal.

Shop Smart: Buy produce in season when it's fresher and less expensive. Look for sales and discounts on plant-based proteins and pantry staples.

Reduce Waste: Minimize food waste by using leftovers creatively in new dishes. For example, turn yesterday's vegetable stir-fry into today's filling for a wrap or omelet.

Plan Ahead: Plan meals in advance to maximize the use of ingredients and minimize waste. Use meal planning to ensure that you have the right ingredients on hand to create diverse and balanced meals throughout the week.

Seek Inspiration: Explore vegetarian cookbooks, online recipes, and cooking blogs to discover new and exciting plant-based dishes that cater to your taste preferences.

By following these tips, you can enjoy the best of both worlds: indulging in quality meat occasionally while embracing an abundance of flavorful, nutritious, and budget-friendly plant-based meals. This balanced approach will not only enhance your well-being but also help reduce the environmental impact of your food choices.

Chapter 41

Unveiling Nutrition Wisdom"

In a world overflowing with fleeting diet trends, the "Sugar Savvy Squad" book stands apart as an enlightening guide that nurtures understanding rather than promoting a fad. Instead of advocating strict rules, it empowers readers with knowledge about nutrition. It doesn't vilify sugar entirely, but rather emphasizes the importance of recognizing the harms of excessive ultra-processed foods and sugar intake. Here's how the book enlightens readers about the complexities of modern diets and the path to better health:

Balanced Perspective on Sugar: The book highlights that sugar isn't all bad, but an excess of it, especially in ultra-processed foods, can contribute to various modern health issues.

Understanding Modern Ailments: By shedding light on the role of sugar and processed foods, the book connects the dots between our diets and modern-day physical and mental afflictions.

Evolution vs. Diet Disruption: It explains how our brains have evolved over time, while our bodies are still adapted to ancestral diets. Processed foods and excessive sugar consumption disrupt this harmony.

Unveiling the Fake Food Issue: The book discusses how our bodies struggle with processing "fake" foods, causing discomfort, mood swings, and health problems.

Return to Cooking: It encourages a return to home cooking, emphasizing that preparing our meals from scratch helps us avoid hidden sugars and unknown additives.

Budget-Friendly Nutrient-Dense Meals:

- Lentil and Vegetable Stew: Packed with protein, fiber, and veggies, this stew is satisfying and cost-effective.
- Quinoa and Black Bean Salad: A protein-rich, nutrient-dense dish that's easy on the wallet.
- Chickpea Curry: A hearty, flavorful meal that's brimming with plant-based protein.
- Oatmeal with Fresh Fruit: A wholesome breakfast option with fiber and natural sweetness.
- Brown Rice Stir-Fry: Load up on vegetables and lean protein for a balanced meal.
- Sweet Potato and Black Bean Tacos: A tasty, low-cost twist on traditional tacos.
- Homemade Veggie Burger: Create your own patties with beans, grains, and veggies.
- Spinach and Cheese Omelet: A protein-packed meal perfect for any time of day.
- Greek Yogurt Parfait: Layer yogurt, fruit, and a sprinkle of nuts for a nutritious dessert or snack.
- Banana omelet, mix one yellow banana with two eggs, fry in olive oil, flip and fold.
- Spinach and mushroom Stroganoff served with quinoa

The "Sugar Savvy Squad" book isn't a fleeting trend but a beacon of wisdom that guides readers toward informed decisions. By advocating for mindful consumption, understanding the impacts of ultra-processed foods, and emphasizing the importance of cooking with whole ingredients, it charts a course to better health and well-being. In a world of noise, this book speaks the language of nourishment, both for the body and the mind.

Dear Readers,

As we come to the end of this transformative journey, I want to express my heartfelt gratitude for joining me on this path to wellness and self-discovery. This book has been a labor of love, and I hope it has ignited a spark within you to embrace positive changes for your health and happiness.

Throughout our exploration, we've learned the power of education and how it equips us with the tools to make informed choices about our well-being. Remember, this is a book of hope—one that shows us that we have the ability to reverse and improve our lives through knowledge and self-awareness.

As we discussed, nutrition plays a crucial role in our health journey, and there are incredible resources out there to deepen our understanding. I encourage you to delve into books written by esteemed nutritionists and doctors, as they offer profound insights and cutting-edge research on health and wellness.

Here is a list of books by top nutritionists and doctors that you can explore:

"The Diet Myth: The Real Science Behind What We Eat" by Tim Spector
"Identically Different: Why We Can Change Our Genes" by Tim Spector
"Spoon-Fed: Why Almost Everything We've Been Told About Food Is Wrong" by Tim Spector
"The Obesity Code: The Diabetes Code and The Cancer Code by Dr. Jason Fung

"The Complete Guide to Fasting: Heal Your Body Through Intermittent, Alternate-Day, and Extended Fasting" by Dr. Jason Fung

"Food: What the Heck Should I Eat?" by Dr. Mark Hyman

"Food Fix: How to Save Our Health, Our Economy, Our Communities, and Our Planet--One Bite at a Time" by Dr. Mark Hyman

"Grain Brain: The Surprising Truth about Wheat, Carbs, and Sugar--Your Brain's Silent Killers" by Dr. David Perlmutter

"How Not to Die: Discover the Foods Scientifically Proven to Prevent and Reverse Disease" by Dr. Michael Greger

"Undo It!: How Simple Lifestyle Changes Can Reverse Most Chronic Diseases" by Dr. Dean Ornish

"The Cholesterol Myth: Heart Health Secrets Revealed" by Dr. Stephen Sinatra

"Reverse Heart Disease Now: Stop Deadly Cardiovascular Plaque Before It's Too Late" by Dr. Stephen Sinatra

"Heart Sense for Women: Your Plan for Natural Prevention and Treatment" by Dr. Stephen Sinatra

"Lower Your Blood Pressure in Eight Weeks: A Revolutionary Program for a Longer, Healthier Life" by Dr. Stephen Sinatra

In addition to these incredible works, there are many more books and resources by experts in the field of nutrition and biochemistry. Explore their writings, listen to their interviews and podcasts, and stay informed about the latest research and discoveries in the realm of nutrition and health.

As you move forward, remember that this journey is not about perfection but progress. Embrace every step, every learning, and every challenge. Cultivate a mindset of self-compassion and celebrate the small victories along the way.

Your health is your greatest asset, and it's worth investing time and effort into nurturing it. Empower yourself with knowledge, make mindful choices, and embark on a life of vitality and fulfillment.

Now, I want to introduce you to two invaluable tools on your continued path to wellness:

Continuous Glucose Monitor (CGM): Consider wearing a CGM to gain deeper insights into how your body responds to different foods. By tracking your blood sugar levels continuously, you can make more informed decisions about your diet and understand how specific foods impact your well-being.

Zoe Science Nutrition: Discover the world of personalized nutrition through Zoe Science Nutrition. They use cutting-edge science to analyze your unique biology and gut health, creating personalized dietary plans tailored to your specific needs and goals.

Finally, I leave you with some inspiring words from Jay Shetty: "Your time is your currency. Invest it wisely." Embrace the journey ahead with courage, hope, and an eagerness to learn. Education is the key to unlocking the doors to a healthier, happier, and more fulfilling life.

Thank you for being part of this extraordinary journey. I wish you a future filled with boundless health, happiness, and the courage to embrace your wellness in all its beautiful forms.

With deep appreciation and warm wishes,

Catherine x

Printed in Great Britain
by Amazon

28391091R00149